AFRICA
ROAD TRIP

1 LANDCRUISER • 2 AUSTRALIANS • 300 DAYS

AFRICA ROAD TRIP

Copyright © C.A. JONES 2014
CreateSpace Edition February 2014
ISBN-13: 978-1495912085

Author: Jones, C.A.
Title: Africa Road Trip

Cover design by Michele Grey
Cover Photograph by B.K. Jones
Book design by Michele Grey

Visit www.jonesroadtrips.com for further information

About the Author

Carol Jones grew up in Sydney, Australia, and following her teacher training set off for Wee Waa in north-west New South Wales for a change from city life and a taste of living 'in the bush'. She has not lived in the city since. Carol and her husband had two boys, chased sheep, went droving, raised cattle and grew a few crops until they left their love of the land for jobs and a few more dollars in the bank. Following a few years in south-west Queensland, the years rolled over back in New South Wales chasing the job opportunities in various towns. In the later years of her teaching career, Carol studied for a Master in Education (Literacy) and specialized in early literacy teaching, while following a keen interest in children's literature. These days she and her husband are chasing their love of traveling and road trips.

Contents

Contents

Prologue

Our hearts are thumping, but we dare not move. Instinctively we all keep still and quiet. We hadn't thought they would come so close!

I whisper to Paul, "Are we alright here?"

He whispers back, "I hope so."

I am sitting on the bonnet of a hired Land Rover Defender in the middle of a sandy riverbed, feeling more vulnerable every second as these giants tread silently closer. My son Paul is next to me leaning against the vehicle. Brian, my husband and Paul's girlfriend Susan are perched up on the roof, cameras ready.

We are in Africa, or more precisely in Damaraland, Namibia. Here in a shimmering dry landscape of scattered trees, Desert Elephants roam up to 70 kilometers a day between hidden waterholes along a branching network of dry river channels. The elephants are notoriously difficult to find, and sightings are treasured.

Already we have spent two days searching before this last early morning run from the Community Campsite on the banks of the Huab River. Two hours have passed and we are ready to concede defeat when suddenly they round a bend some distance away. They approach in single file up on the bank of the river, three or four adults shepherding the juveniles and babies.

Brian hits the brakes. We are ecstatic to see the elusive creatures but want the best view possible. Knowing that the vegetation beside the river will hide them as they pass by, we retreat a short distance around another bend of the river, and wait.

Eager to make the most of the imminent photo opportunity, Brian and Susan clamber onto the roof of the vehicle, cameras in hand. Tingling with anticipation, we are aware of every sound and movement in the quiet of the bush surrounding us – from a rustling leaf to the occasional twittering bird – we wait for the elephants to come back into sight.

But no, this is not part of the plan. They were supposed to stay up on the bank and parade past us at a safe distance. Now they are using our vehicle tracks down in the riverbed as their path. They are heading directly for us!

The leading matriarch spies us ahead, and stops briefly to work us out. Apparently she decides we are not a threat – it is elephant territory after all – and that it is unnecessary to lead her group back up along the river bank to avoid us. The elephants come closer. It is too late to contemplate a dash into the car and a quick getaway. Elephants have been known to charge if panicked. We are mesmerized, but feeling exposed so close to the bulk of wrinkled skin, gently waving ears and steady eyes silently approaching. We freeze, and even the clicking of cameras above me has stopped.

The elephants are only a triple jump away, stirring up the desert sand dust as they pass, the youngsters protected in amongst sturdy legs. Just as we are starting to breathe more freely, the last elephant halts unexpectedly and turns her head our way. We hold a collective breath. She looks hard at us and before moving on sweeps her trunk towards us and trumpets as if to say, *Better watch out!* and continues to swagger on by.

We know we have experienced something magical, but mixed in with the euphoria of the moment is an understanding of the unpredictability of animals in the wild and the realization that we had unintentionally put ourselves in grave danger. But our utter enchantment with the African continent materializes from that point onwards.

It is 2008 and my husband Brian and I are on a six-week camping trip with our son Paul and his girlfriend Susan through Zambia, Botswana and Namibia. It is during this time that the seed of a grand plan for a future trip is sown, and snowballs in our minds.

Why can't we ship our own vehicle from Australia? It is roadworthy, reliable and we know its history and we can set it up for camping in Africa. Why not drive north from somewhere in South Africa and visit the countries on the eastern side of the continent all the way up to Europe? Why not? We are towards the end of our working careers. Time is on our side and we can travel to a time frame of our choice. Twelve months? Maybe more. We can play it all by ear. All the decisions are ours.

An affordable camping adventure seems possible, doable and exciting. The more we chat about it up in our roof tent, the more feasible it becomes. Why not next year? Why wait? Surprisingly, the idea has lost none of its appeal by the time we return to Australia and are back in the everydayness of work and life. Our first sounding boards are our children. Their reaction is all we need. "Go for it!"

Others are not so sure. Mystified looks are the norm and the repeated question, "Will you be safe?"

What are we thinking? Can we really do this alone?

Brian is always supremely confident and optimistic, but feelings of doubt creep into my consciousness. We love the freedom of traveling independently, but should we travel with others for safety in numbers?

Will we be safe?

Just over twelve months later in 2009, we ship our vehicle from Sydney to Durban, and travel through South Africa, Swaziland, Lesotho, Namibia, Botswana, Zambia, Malawi, Mozambique, Tanzania, Rwanda, Uganda, Kenya, Ethiopia, Sudan, Egypt, Libya and Tunisia. A ferry from Tunisia to Palermo in Sicily celebrates the completion of our African continent adventure.

1.

Elephant Obsession

The sheer size of an elephant makes every encounter an awe-inspiring experience, further intensified when a herd comes into view. Elephants possess a powerful presence even in a wide expansive African landscape. It is elephants that create one of the highlights of our journey through Southern and East Africa.

In Etosha National Park, Namibia, much of the wildlife viewing is at the waterholes scattered across the 4730 square kilometer pan, originally a lake that dried up millions of years ago. All three rest camps across Etosha provide the opportunity to sight wildlife as they come in to water, but Okaukuejo Rest Camp excels. A variety of wildlife congregates around this waterhole any time of night or day. White and black rhinoceros, giraffes, lions and elephants appear at night, illuminated by spotlights, while during the day the plains animals – zebra, wildebeest, springbok and gemsbok (oryx) – jostle for drinking or resting positions. There is a continual stream of animals arriving and departing.

On the viewing side of the waterhole there is always a hush so as not to frighten anything away, while on the wildlife side the dynamics between the species unfold as predators and their prey alike seem to know when to approach, though occasionally there is a frantic scatter if the timing is not quite right.

We visit the more remote waterholes off the tourist loop. Luck is a major factor when it comes to any sighting. It all depends on random decisions such as to take one track and not the other, or to leave too early, or unluckily to just arrive too late and be told of all the excitement just missed.

Our fascination with elephants finds new heights one day when we chance upon a herd, with babies and adolescents, all taking part in a frenzied mud bath, a mere puddle of water following some recent rain. By the time we arrive, it is black and muddy from all the furious activity which continues while we sit in the vehicle completely captivated. *Are we too close?* We feel safe in our vehicle, but just how safe are we? Thirty meters will be no comfort in the path of an angry ear-flapping, snorting matriarch.

The elephants are deliriously enjoying the inches-deep puddle, rolling around, lying, kneeling or standing in it, squirting themselves and others, smothering themselves in the mud with their trunks doubling as spatulas to make sure that as much of their huge frame as possible is covered in mud. They trumpet, and grunt and splash, and the rank odor of wet bodies and what is now putrid mud wafts in our direction. When a few start walking our way we feel a tinge of panic. Brian starts the engine ready to retreat, but it is not our vehicle in their sights, but the dry dusty earth which they pick up with their trunks and toss over their shining wet bodies. We leave them in peace, not wanting to test the situation, enthralled by our lucky encounter.

★★★

Our New South Wales (NSW), Australian registered vehicle with its black on yellow number plate is confusing for many travelers along the way, perhaps because the word Australia is nowhere to be seen. The word Wales should mean Wales, so perhaps it is easy to ignore the preceding two words and assume we are Welsh, which happens a few times. The 'AUS' circular sticker on the back of the car has been issued by the Australian Automobile Association, with 'AAA' written in small print underneath, but the larger print 'AUS' is often mistaken for Austria, another common conclusion. We think our kangaroo sticker on the back is a dead give-away, but we have made the decision to be less conspicuous with a small and discreet kangaroo, so dead give-away it is not.

Jaques and Mandy, however, recognize our number plate immediately and are incredulous. Their Toyota Troopie (Troop Carrier) displays the same black and yellow New South Wales license plate even though they are from South Africa. A young couple, they have traveled widely together. They worked in the UK for a number of years and then traveled to Australia, visiting the east coast and the Center. Back in Sydney, they decided to buy a vehicle to drive back to South Africa, and now they are nearly home. We are inspired – and here we all are, two Toyotas with New South Wales number plates on the Luangwa River in Zambia!

Croc Valley Camp in Zambia sits on the banks of the Luangwa River across from the South Luangwa National Park. The river's reduced flow due to the dry season allows wildlife to cross from the National Park so it is an exhilarating place to camp. The grass is continually watered by the Croc Valley staff, presumably for the benefit of the campers, but the fresh green pick is a constant attraction to wildlife.

Late in the afternoon on our first day, an elephant passes between our camper and a tree a mere two meters away, treating our camper as part of the landscape. Shaun, the owner, had warned us on arrival to be wary of hippos at night, and elephants day and night. Now we already know he did not exaggerate.

Asleep in our camper that evening, we are suddenly wide awake and listening to a strange and unfamiliar sound. We stealthily climb out of bed to peep out of the windows. There below us in the darkness, and just centimeters from our elevated camper, a huge hippopotamus quietly munches on the grass.

The hippopotamus is not listed as one of the African Big Five Game Species, a term coined in the era of big game hunting for trophies. Lion, elephant, buffalo, leopard and rhinoceros are considered the most difficult and dangerous to hunt on foot, with a high degree of danger involved irrespective of their size. Despite their omission from the Big Five, hippos are responsible for many human deaths in Africa and are regarded as highly dangerous and aggressive, easily capable of outrunning a human. We have read that most victims are caught between the hippo and deep water or between a mother and her calf.

This hippo is so close, we dare not even whisper, but he is unperturbed by our trespass onto his turf and is intent on eating the sweet grass along the river bank. Elated to be within the realm of this much revered and feared African animal, we gaze through the shadows watching him as he gradually moves away on his quest to feed that enormous body.

★★★

Campsites throughout Southern Africa have bars, often open air with a fabulous atmosphere. While we chat to other travelers, a sundowner, usually a beer or a wine, is an irresistible part of the day. One evening it is well after dusk when we make our way from the Croc Valley bar that overlooks the river back to our camp fifty meters further along the bank. We are strolling along feeling relaxed, having thoroughly enjoyed the ambience under the beautiful sunset colors of an African sky when, not far from our camp, we hear some commotion to our right near the restaurant. In the dimness we make out an elephant, rushing around looking agitated. Brian grabs my arm. With a jolt we grasp the situation. Here, out in the open, we are defenseless. We sprint to our camp and scuttle inside, puffing and sizing up our position as we anxiously gape through the windows. *Are we safe in here?* Our camper is elevated on our vehicle, but how safe is that from a rampaging member of the African Big Five? We watch in disbelief as the elephant charges towards the open-air thatched restaurant, the diners fleeing to the back in a wave of fear. The elephant stops just short of climbing the couple of steps at the entrance. As we fretfully peer through the shadows, we wonder, will our camper be regarded as an easier target? Even at this distance, it is alarming to watch. Eventually, some brave camp employees appear and calmly distract the elephant. He drifts in our direction. We hold our breaths, paralyzed with anxiety, until at last he heads towards the river. We can't believe how stupid we were. How could we have let down our guard so completely walking back from the bar?

★★★

Croc Valley has a swimming pool for those hot days when the 'no-swim' river teases for a refreshing dip. After a hippo ended up in the pool a couple of years ago and had to be destroyed despite all efforts to free it, the pool was re-fashioned with a gentle slope to the middle. The depth is now only a meter or so, but as Shaun recounts in his 'Elephants in the Pool' story, it can still be a hazard for wildlife.

A female elephant, two juveniles and a baby walked through the camp and then all stopped to drink at the pool. The baby walked in a little way to drink, but then slipped further in and couldn't get out. So the mother went in, and the two juveniles followed, which meant there were four elephants in the pool. The mother walked out, but the baby couldn't manage the slippery slope, so the mother became angry and distressed, and attacked and wrecked the little wooden structure housing the pool filter. Eventually, the mother wrapped her trunk around the baby and with the aid of the juveniles they managed to help the baby out of the pool. The mother and baby took off and one of the juveniles walked out of the pool, but the other couldn't get out, leaving one elephant in the pool. As the story goes, the mother elephant came back and was rampaging around again, so Shaun had to get a rifle and fire a shot into the air, as pool chairs were suffering the vent of her anger, and who was to know what would be next? The mother left, but there was still one elephant in the pool. So the staff managed to get a tarpaulin around the back of the youngster like a sling, and hauled him out, men scattering left and right after the rescue when the juvenile elephant set off in pursuit of his family. Shaun added that the next time he painted the pool floor he planned to mix some sand into the paint to provide better grip for thirsty visitors.

2.

The Planning – a canvas penthouse, red tape and visas, and bon voyage to the LandCruiser

Nothing quite compares to sleeping under canvas to the symphony of an all-encompassing African night, but the roar of a lion within meters of the camp must be disconcerting at ground level. The benefit of sleeping at a comfortable height above the ground becomes blatantly clear in our roof tent experiences with Paul and Susan in 2008.

For years we have been keen on the Trayon, manufactured in Maroochydore, on the Queensland Sunshine Coast in Australia. We love the concept of a compact unit on the tray-top of our Toyota LandCruiser, which is completely secure when folded up, and looks like a big white box similar to a small refrigeration unit. The Trayon sits comfortably on the back, with room for the two spare tires behind the cab. When the roof opens out it becomes the bed within a comfortable and self-contained little 'house' under a canvas cover. And the bed is two meters off the ground. Perfect!

There are two built-in seats and a table, an Engel upright fridge, a sink, a gas stove-top and cupboards, as well as an emergency toilet hidden away in a cupboard under one of the seats. There is a gas hot water system for the sink and for an outside shower. The purchase of such 'luxury' camping equipment was supposed to wait until sleeping on the ground in a tent had become a chore rather than good fun, many years down the track. But now it seems a good idea to bring the purchase forward.

★★★

We haven't always been campers. Our very first four wheel drive was a Nissan Patrol, bought originally for towing horses to pony camps and local shows with our two sons, Craig and Paul. So our first camping experience was in the swept-out horse float sleeping in Australian swags of rolled-up bedding.

Camping and fishing adventures followed in school holidays. Fraser Island and Moreton Island which both lie off the coast of Queensland were our favorite destinations. After packing all our camping gear in the back of the Nissan or on the roof rack – fishing gear, tents, swags, firewood, water – we could barely find room to fit food and drinks. We thought we had only the bare essentials, but with four passengers and all of our gear, the vehicle was bursting at the seams.

The very first time we drove onto sand on Fraser Island we were a little anxious. We were used to rough roads – unsealed, corrugated, sandy, or sticky with black mud after rain – but driving on sand on a beach was a new experience. It was high tide as the barge pulled in and the dry deep sand ahead looked ominous. Brian revved the engine, and with tires deflated we powered off the deck, bouncing around the vehicle and hanging on until we reached the firm track through the beach scrub. No problems, other than everything in the vehicle had found a new location.

Years later we bought our single cab Toyota LandCruiser tray-top, with camping for two in mind. Our boys were launching new lives in Sydney, six hours drive from our home in Tamworth in north-west New South Wales, Australia, so we prepared ourselves for a camping holiday through the Simpson Desert. Our new Cruiser had dual battery, a winch, two long range fuel tanks of 90 liters each, a 25 liter tank for drinking water, and two more water tanks which could hold up to 160 liters. We traded the new standard tires for six new BF Goodrich All Terrain tires and we transferred our comfortable Paratus driver's seat into the new Toyota and invested in one for the passenger seat as well. Paratus seats are designed for travel comfort and have a hand pump to inflate the lumber support, which is a bonus after a long day rattling on bumpy roads. All our camping gear was thrown in the covered tray behind.

The Simpson Desert and surrounding landscapes were awe-inspiring. It was a 600 kilometer drive traveling west to east across the rolling, red sand dunes, 1100 dunes running north to south. Our tall orange flag mounted on the roo bar was the only warning to oncoming vehicles that we were approaching a dune summit on the single lane track, unless we managed to make contact with other travelers on our UHF radio. It was early days for GPS technology, but we had our Mio PDA (Personal Digital Assistant) which had limited GPS capabilities and came with

Australian maps, though lacking detail in the Simpson. On our last day, after climbing Big Red, the final massive sand dune, we stayed at the Birdsville Hotel and toasted our triumph. Perhaps this was where the seed of a grand plan for overland travel had really been sown.

★★★

Over the next twelve months or so we fit out the new Trayon camper into a comfortable but tiny home. Food and utensils are squeezed into the nooks and crannies under the kitchen bench. Our clothes are stowed into cupboards below, no bigger than cabin luggage, so our wardrobe fills quickly. The shoe cupboard is under our feet under the table. The bookshelf above is our library. Another small space snugly houses two bulky warm coats and sleeping bags just in case a hotel bed looks suspect. Our first aid kit takes the place of shoes we now don't need and the last available cupboard becomes our office, storing a computer and electronics. The bedroom is easy with no hard decisions. When the roof folds out, there is the bed.

Everything on board contributes to the overall weight and takes up valuable space, so every single item is the subject of much thought and discussion. We even joke about taking stickers off items to save weight! There is little space for such things as souvenirs along the road, a case in point when we are in Outjo, a dusty town at the gateway to Etosha in Namibia. It's quite touristy with coffee shops and numerous gift shops with African artifacts, but we resist, having bought our carved hippo and giraffe on our previous visit. The Kudu leather shoes tempt Brian, but the shoe cupboard is full!

Our little abode has all we need. But my mind plays with vivid worst case scenarios of being stranded on lonely roads, or busy city-street breakdowns amongst loud shouting and tooting horns. What is the balance between carrying numerous spare parts and the probability of mechanical problems? Nowhere can be found the perfect answer! Opinions vary widely, every vehicle is different, every planned journey unique. The bare minimum is our answer, knowing it is impossible to cover all risks. We have a reliable vehicle, so we put our faith in the Cruiser and find space for fan belts, radiator hoses, oil and fuel filters, two tire tubes, tire changing gear and a tire repair kit. Essential tools and an assortment of fuses, nuts and bolts, electrical tape and all the other bits and pieces critical to any worthwhile toolbox, such as plenty of cable ties, are all thrown in. We have read that spare parts can be shipped and delivered within days worldwide via DHL and similar companies. Yes, a very expensive option but a good back up and possibly better than never-to-be-used extra weight on board.

Some modifications are made to our Cruiser. We upgrade to Old Man Emu suspension, as well as installing two suspension air bags under the tray to support the weight of the camper. 'ARB' diff locks are also added to the rear wheels of the vehicle. Diff locks are an extra weapon to combat difficult terrain, locking the rear wheels to create more traction. A high-lift jack is purchased and secured to the head-rail behind the cab.

Finally, inside the cab we fit a center-floor compartment console between the Paratus seats, and a 'shelf roof' console above the windscreen so that maps, books and other possessions can be kept out of sight at all times. A security system with automatic immobilization is also installed. With the great unknown ahead, it seems a good idea to safeguard our home and transport.

★★★

We purchase a Garmin Oregon GPS. Paul had told us all about the Tracks 4 Africa maps on our first African camping trip together. These maps are compiled by a community of travelers throughout Africa who record and share points of interest ranging from attractions to fuel stops, and they include accommodation options for the overland traveler, especially campsites.

Tracks 4 Africa maps enable us to plan our itinerary north from Durban through the whole African continent on the computer at home. It is possible to choose campsites at realistic intervals knowing full well that this is just a plan and when we are on the ground many other options will materialize. But in the planning stage, to see the route mapped out within a reasonable time frame is very re-assuring. We are starting to feel we can do this! There it is on our computer. Yet we know that a track on a map reveals nothing of what we will encounter. Pangs of anxiety mixed with excitement surface frequently.

Our communication strategy is planned. We take an extra phone handset for our Travel Sim, and our own phones for emergencies and for swapping local sim cards for even cheaper local calls. We enquire about satellite phones before we leave but there is not one that will work both in Africa and in Australia so we will research a satellite phone when we arrive in Africa. We take the computer for Skype, our blog and to stay in touch with family via email, and we plan to purchase data on USB modems available from Telcos all over Africa.

★★★

The Carnet de Passage is a crucial document, essential for overland travel through Africa, and necessary at all border crossings. It shows engine and chassis number and declares that the vehicle has been exported from Australia and will be imported back into Australia at a later date. The carnet is only available from the Automobile Association of Australia in Canberra through the National Roads and Motorists' Association (NRMA).

Comprehensive insurance is totally out of the question and third party insurance is the best that can be hoped for when driving overland in Africa. In South Africa, Namibia and Botswana, third party insurance is covered in the price of fuel and in the rest of the African countries south of Egypt, the Yellow Card Insurance is available. In Egypt and Libya, third party insurance is covered in the registration process and in Tunisia we will get insurance on the border. Finally, we will need a Green Card for Europe which we will organize closer to our date of arrival.

Driving a New South Wales registered vehicle overseas could be problematic if we are away for over twelve months and need to re-register the vehicle. We contact the Road Traffic Authority (RTA NSW) and after abundant correspondence they inform us re-registration will be possible if the pink slip is filled in by a government transport agency overseas. The pink slip is used as a check list for vehicle roadworthiness in NSW. This sounds reasonable and possible, but months later in Egypt when we embark on this mission, it is neither.

★★★

We are planning to travel through seventeen countries on the African continent, so research into visa requirements is ongoing from the start of planning. We email some of the consulates and embassies, we visit web sites and with further research it appears that for most countries, Australians either do not need visas or can secure them at border crossings.

Sudan is one of the exceptions and is a major concern to us. In the Sudan Bradt guidebook we read about George of the Pagoulatos family, originally from Greece who can help with all the paperwork and visas. The Pagoulatos family runs a tourism venture based around the Acropole Hotel in Khartoum. Before we leave Australia, we make contact with George by email and he is helpful and reassuring. Everything we need can be processed through George. He will contact the Department of Tourism in Sudan and his introduction will allow our entry into the country. All will be taken care of. Our visas for Sudan can be picked up in Addis Ababa in Ethiopia.

We also believe that Libya may be difficult. We email Arkno Tours Information Office in London which organizes tours of Libya. Their suggestion is to have an Arabic translation of the first page of the passport inserted at the back of our passports for ease of travel into and throughout Libya. They give us the name and contact details of a certified translator in Canberra, Australia. We make contact with her, send our passports down by registered post and receive our back page translation in under a fortnight, for a fee of course. Arkno Tours also informs us of costs associated with guided travel in Libya, which appears to be the only choice. We will have to pay for customs clearance, visas, passport registration, travel permits, a daily fee for a guide, as well as guide transfers and accommodation. It all seems too hard and far too expensive at this planning stage, so once again we decide that we can always go through Syria and Jordan as an alternative, or perhaps meet up with other travelers along the way to share a guide and save costs. Libyan visas will have to be secured while traveling and they do prove to be the most frustrating of all – but that saga doesn't unfold until we are in Egypt.

In the quest for our Egyptian visas we first visit the premises of the Egypt Consulate General at Surry Hills in Sydney to be assured that Australians can get the required visa on the border when entering. Given that the visas are valid only for six months from date of issue to time of entry, we have no choice but to accept this advice.

★★★

Our local GP has an interest in and in-depth knowledge of travel medicine and provides measured and thoughtful advice on a range of medical issues. Larium is the recommended choice for protection against malaria due to the extended nature of our travel through malarial areas. She also recommends a number of vaccinations including Hep B, Hep A, Typhoid, Polio, Rabies, Cholera, Yellow Fever, Pneumonia and Flu. Our GP also helps us compile a first aid kit with only the essentials, which include a well thought-out number of bandages and dressings, burn treatments, syringes and needles, antibiotics, and medication for self-treatment of the hard-to-avoid travelers' diarrhea.

Our doctor also stresses vigilance with drinking water and even dish-washing water. We invest in a water pump and a filter system to ensure any water pumped into our camper is safe for cooking and washing dishes. We also have iodine to treat water from any questionable source. We plan to buy all our drinking water. Finally, we get travel insurance with Defense Health and an all–clear from the dentist.

★★★

We choose Cargo Online as our freight forwarder. They have good agents in Durban and we find them good to deal with from their Sydney office. We ship to Durban rather than Cape Town because it is a much larger port and we visited beautiful Cape Town and the surrounding area when Paul and Susan were living and working there.

Shipping a vehicle is not a cheap option, but hiring or buying an unknown vehicle and fitting it out in an unfamiliar country could be problematic and not a cheap option in the long term for a journey of the length we are planning. Hiring a Land Rover for six weeks on our last trip to Africa incurred a similar cost to shipping our own vehicle from Sydney to Durban.

★★★

We hear of a mature-aged local adventurer who has a property not far from Tamworth. He has driven solo through many countries in Africa over a number of visits. We contact him and he is happy for us to visit and chat with him about his adventures. He shows us his old battered Toyota Troopie parked in the shed, testament to the rough roads and tracks experienced all over Africa including the west coast. He shares some of his tips for Africa such as to forget about insurance; where to hide cash in the vehicle; and not to give the locals a ride in the car because it is too risky. I'm feeling nervous again. He also tells us he has never eaten the local food! On each of his trips he carried tinned and dried food with him. I do have a worry list, but sampling the culinary delights of each country is not on it and I don't want to add it now.

★★★

For a trial run of our camper we spend a week on Moreton Island with Paul and Susan, who now live back in Australia. The camper successfully weathers the howling winds and rain from a cyclone further north. The only further modification needed is a tweaking of the battery wiring system.

In mid-May, six weeks before our flight to Africa, we drive the vehicle from Tamworth to Botany Bay in Sydney to be loaded into a shipping container in readiness for its journey to Durban.

Strangely, standard shipping containers still measure length imperially at 20 feet long, yet measure height in metric at 2.2 meters. Our Cruiser with the camper on top makes for an excruciatingly tight squeeze, even with all the air out of the suspension air bags, and reduced pressure in the tires. An employee drives the vehicle into the container and emerges from between the back wheels with great difficulty.

"You'd be pleased to be out of there!" we comment, only to be told good humouredly that he has to crawl back in later to chock the wheels and tie it all down.

Now we really feel the journey has begun. We are committed, and there is no turning back. Our vehicle is on its way and we must follow. Most of our packing is complete, with the bulk of our clothing on its way in the camper. Hand luggage, computers and cameras are left to carry on to the plane. Only our imagination sees what lies ahead. We will need resilience and no doubt some courage at times. My nerves still niggle, but no, we haven't packed a gun!

3.

Will You Be Safe?

"Will you be safe?" So many times we are asked this question before leaving home. And even, "Are you taking a gun?"

We are acutely aware as we drive along that we have more possessions in our vehicle and camper than many of the people we are seeing along the way will have in their entire lifetime. And, to us, this is the bare minimum of possessions. It is a disturbing thought.

For the entire journey we exercise the greatest of caution. When we pull up at a campsite, we immediately lock the driver's side while we set up camp on the passenger side. In Dar Es Salaam, Tanzania, an English couple with whom we later travel through Kenya, have money and passports stolen from the front seat of their vehicle while they are chatting with fellow campers on the other side.

Habitually we travel with our passenger doors locked. Nothing is carried as we walk through towns or tourist attractions

– we use hidden pockets always close to the body – and wear no jewelery, not even watches. I carry a small camera in a pocket, and the SLR only surfaces where we feel comfortable using it. We carry very little money on our person, which is possible because ATMs are relatively easy to find, and always have an English language option. In Sudan, however, there are none, and in Rwanda and Libya they are a challenge. We keep US dollars and euros for use in any emergency or for when we are caught without local money. We always go together to an ATM and if we feel uncomfortable because it is in too quiet a street or people are loitering around, we find another one. Our favorites are those housed inside the banks.

One of the things we love about our Cruiser and camper is the fact that we don't really look touristy, not at first glance anyway, until of course we are visible sitting inside, by which time we have driven past. When the vehicle is parked and left on its own, it certainly arouses some curiosity, and undoubtedly is picked as a tourist vehicle, but it is not blatantly obvious. Our security system gives us more confidence when leaving it unattended. Our white box is interpreted to be many different things, and we are always asked at border crossings just what we are carrying inside. Rarely do we have to open it up any further than unlocking the steps and putting them down, and after peering inside, where the fridge and cupboards are about all that can be deciphered in the gloom, the border officials send us on our way.

Traveling solo in our own vehicle suits us perfectly, and the freedom to please ourselves is enormously appealing. In Africa we are not good bush campers, preferring the security of a proper campsite, often with on-site security guards. Later, when there is a case for 'safety in numbers', we travel with others and thoroughly enjoy the company. There are definitely benefits to traveling with others but for extended travel over many months, independence is our choice.

It is not long before we realize that the greatest risk on a journey of this sort is a road accident. It appears that crazy drivers are everywhere, taking enormous risks overtaking on hills and curves with zero visibility, merely trusting their luck. On the other hand when the road is flat with clear visibility, it seems the plan is to test the mettle of the oncoming driver by overtaking and squeezing in with only a paper-thin margin to spare. Paper-thin margin mistakes abandoned on the side of the road tend to moderate pressure on the accelerator and we find that our general speed rarely exceeds 90 kilometers per hour even under the best conditions.

★★★

A definite highlight of our African journey is the fellow overlanders we meet at the campsites. We had not expected to meet so many people traveling in their own or hired vehicles, let alone the wealth of campsites along the way. Africa is a well traveled continent, mainly due to the number of tourists seeking adventure with guided overland trucks, which are sturdy and bus-like and pick up and drop off tourists over the full length of Africa, depending on the adventure they seek. They camp in tents along the way and most are craving wildlife, but there is so much to see in Africa and the overland trucks can be seen everywhere. Consequently the campsites cater for these trucks because it is an important part of their business. Some overland travelers in their own vehicles dislike camping alongside the trucks, because they mean more people and more noise, but we find it intriguing and enjoy chatting to the travelers. Brian regularly strikes up conversations with the local drivers and tour guides, who know all the good campsites and if approached good-naturedly are happy to share their knowledge.

Most fellow overlanders driving independently are from Europe – France, Germany, The Netherlands, Spain, Italy, Norway, Sweden, Poland, Switzerland and Austria, but also from the UK and Ireland, South Africa and two couples from Australia. We also meet motorbike riders from Israel, Egypt and the UK, and cyclists from Germany, Austria and Switzerland. As many of these are like-minded people, friendships are quickly and easily formed, and if we meet again further along the track, it feels like they are long lost friends.

★★★

Initially, in the early stages of our journey we promise ourselves a 'no-rules journey', with on-the-run decision-making the norm. However, eventually we do set ourselves three rules: 1) don't drive too far in one day; 2) cross borders in the mornings, not in the afternoons; 3) never walk or drive at night.

Despite best intentions, we break every one of our self-imposed rules on our 'no-rules-journey-with-rules', even all three in the same day on one occasion. Our comfort zone is regularly challenged and broadened.

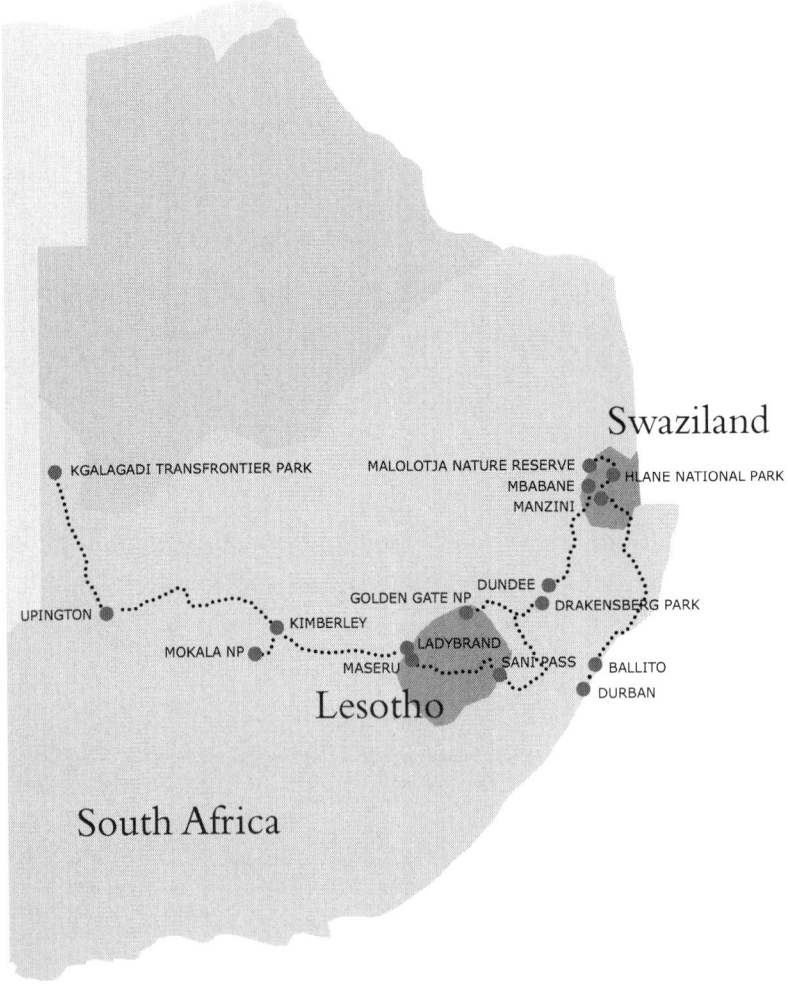

4.

South Africa – on the road and camping, Zulus and wild animals

In Durban we fill in five days as we wait and pine for our vehicle. The LandCruiser has arrived but numerous bureaucratic hoops need to be jumped through before it can be released from its shackles. Loads of patience is required and our sight-seeing is peppered with regular phone calls to our freight forwarders.

A city tour seems like a good idea. When we check with the receptionist at the hotel, she smilingly volunteers to organize it all for us which also seems like a good idea. However, contrary to our expectations of a tourist company sending a mini bus or car, as it turns out the receptionist's cousin (they are both of Indian descent) arrives in a very ramshackle car with worn out seats, hit and miss door handles, and a few personal belongings quickly shoved out of the way. Manoj is a friendly personable fellow, who offers to take us wherever we want to go in Durban. We ask him a few questions, including the price, and accept his offer that will most likely provide a different experience from a regular organized tour.

Manoj tells us a great deal about Durban from his perspective, especially elaborating on the changes to life in the city since the African National Congress (ANC) came to power in 1994. The Durban of today is a bubbling city of streets more crowded with shoppers than cars. This vibrant shopping frenzy is mostly black Africans who know they pay less for goods in Central Durban than out in the malls in the surrounding suburbs which are frequented by the middle classes, both black and white. In contrast during Apartheid in South Africa, the sedate and colonial city center was frequented by mostly whites and Indians. Manoj shows us City Hall, once the venue for big events and sophisticated audiences, but now boarded up. The surrounding parks look neglected and dirty and an old statue of a Victorian statesman is adorned with a discarded hat in what seems to be a mockery of bygone days. Manoj discloses his preference for the Apartheid days but the atmosphere of life being led by the busy local population seems fitting to us. He takes us to the Victoria Embankment, Wilsons Wharf, the busy Victoria Street Market and to the huge suburban shopping malls in the suburbs. We visit glorious Durban beaches, and walk along the Golden Mile. We are guided through a Hindu Temple and he even suggests a couple of Indian restaurants we could try that evening. Our tour with Manoj is a success.

The next day we find the recommended Oriental Restaurant in The Workshop, a shopping center constructed from an old Victorian building which was once a railway workshop. Judging by the restaurant's popularity we presume the food must be good, but it is early days in our travels and on this occasion we lack the confidence to mix it with the locals vying for a seat in a very cramped space. In retrospect we should have eaten there, and in just a few weeks time we are no longer phased by these situations. This day we opt instead for lunch at an Indian restaurant 'Jewel of India' within a hotel along the esplanade across from the beach. It caters more for tourists than locals, but serves up great Indian food all the same.

★★★

The day of our reunion with our Cruiser has arrived. Thomas from the freight forwarders picks us up after lunch from our hotel and drives us to the Port of Durban where he deposits us in a small office. We wait … and wait. A yawning, sleepy but pleasant, female Zulu Customs Officer eventually arrives with Thomas and we all drive to the container which is sitting near the dock outside a warehouse. The lock is first checked to see that it hasn't been tampered with, and the door is opened. And there is our Cruiser, our close companion for the coming months, safe and sound and sitting snugly in his cramped seafaring cabin. Yes, our Cruiser is definitely a 'he' we have decided. He will need brute strength, muscle power and tenacity for the mission ahead. So we have named him Bruno. And now we cannot wait to climb aboard and be on our way. But no! Not so fast. The carnet and all the official documents still need to be stamped and signed by all the officials who are required to stamp and sign them. We also need to finalize our paperwork with Thomas and pay the last of numerous extra little fees. We are tantalizingly close. It is 3.15 pm. But now we are told that the vehicle cannot be released until tomorrow! We are in Africa and we are starting to understand the waiting game.

The following morning we are driven straight to Bruno, now draped in glorious southern hemisphere sunshine, reminiscent of home. We are free! We drive our very first African kilometers back to the hotel full of anticipation and eager to be on our way.

★★★

At last we are on the road heading north out of Durban! This is Zulu country with small African villages, larger towns and very rich agricultural land with sugar cane and pineapples in stalls beside the road. We spend two nights at a campsite at Ballito on the Kwa Zulu-Natal Coast, a popular seaside holiday destination on a coastline of beautiful rocky outcrops and small beaches. Looking back we could have spent more time there, but we are so keen to launch into the real adventure ahead that a coastal holiday environment is not so high on our list of priorities.

The historic battlefields on the black soil plains around Dundee are where the early Zulu wars, Zulu–Boer battles, Zulu–British battles, Boer–British battles and numerous uprisings and rebellions were all fought. It looks like country worth fighting for. The beautiful open grassland amongst scattered hills hides rich and fertile soil.

The site of the battle of the Voortrekkers (Boers) against the mighty Zulu army in 1838 is the only one of its kind in South Africa as the two sides have interpreted the battle quite differently. The Blood River Heritage Site presents the battle from the Boer perspective in contrast to the Zulu perspective presented at Ncome Museum. Even the accounts of historians vary.

Essentially, the story reveals that the Boers visited the Zulu King Dingane to negotiate the purchase of land, but according to the Zulu culture, an uninvited visit to their king was a declaration of war. On a final visit, the Boer leader Piet Retief and his comrades were killed on the command of the Zulu king and in follow-up attacks hundreds of other Boers were massacred by the Zulus. In the final battle, the Boers strategically placed their wagons on the banks of the Ncome River, and the Zulus attacked with between 12,000 and 15,000 warriors. The Zulus launched attack after attack but to no avail, and eventually started to retreat. The Boers countered with a mounted pursuit and killed three thousand Zulu warriors but only lost three of their men, including their new leader Andries Pretorius. Hence, the Ncome River is often referred to as the Blood River.

An open air memorial at the Blood River Heritage Site comprises 60 bronze wagons, a replica of the laager (D-shape) formation that the Boers used to defend themselves against the Zulus. On the other hand, the Ncome Museum is architecturally unique in that it takes its shape from the Zulu war horn formation initiated by Zulu King Shaka.

★★★

Golden Gate National Park in South Africa is so called for the golden color of the cliff formations which also display beautiful red and yellow colors at different times of day, and unusual erosion patterns with the granite deposits throughout the sandstone. Here we spend two of our coldest nights – minus 1.2 degrees Celsius in the camper on the first morning is cold enough, but the second morning is minus 4.6 degrees Celsius!

The fridge temperature is minus 1.2 so we would have been warmer in there! Our water bottles are frozen even though they are not in the fridge. Iced brown bananas and a crunchy dishcloth are on the sink. We cook eggs to warm the camper and ourselves.

The next day on arrival at the gateway to Giant's Castle in the Drakensberg Mountains, we are not too disappointed to be told by the ranger that camping is not permitted. At a height of 3315 meters compared to 1823 meters back at Golden Gate, we are happy to find a lower altitude haven for the night.

★★★

In Mokala National Park our campsite is situated on a watering hole where we watch zebra, tsessebe and warthogs come in to water. We are sharing our game-viewing campsite at Haak en Steek with three South African couples. "Are you really from Australia?" is now a common question. We share and view each other's camping set-ups, and it isn't long before we are listening to their radio tuned into a South Africa versus Australia rugby match. Australia loses. They are ecstatic and really rub it in. It's hard, but they redeem themselves by inviting us to a delicious campsite meal of *sosaties* (meat marinated on skewers), and *boervurss* sausage cooked on the *braii* (barbecue) with mixed vegetables cooked in olive oil and rosemary. They also share their Aussie jokes with us. Great! One joke goes something like this:

An Australian is driving an American around his property. A steer runs across the road.

American: What's that?

Australian: A steer.

American: We call that a calf!

Next a horse crosses in front of them.
American: What's that?
Australian: A horse.
American: We call that a foal!
Finally a kangaroo jumps across the road.
American: What's that?
Australian: A grasshopper. What do you call it?

★★★

The town of Kimberley is known for its Big Hole. The discovery of diamonds 150 years ago led to the largest hand-dug excavation in the world and the start of the De Beers diamond venture. By the time mining ended in 1914 the mine yielded 2722 kilograms of diamonds from 22.5 million tons of excavated earth.

The Big Hole today is a massive crater, 214 meters deep in the middle of Kimberley, filled with eerie dark turquoise-blue water. We speak with a local as we wander around who tells us he used to go there as a boy and throw stones over the edge. These days the sides are caving in and access has been restricted to the huge platform constructed above the hole. We explore the 'old town' with its reconstructed period buildings but find it very touristy, and leave without any diamond souvenirs!

★★★

We have our first puncture while traveling west towards the Kgalagadi Transfrontier Park, a large wildlife preserve and conservation area in southern Africa which straddles the border between South Africa and Botswana, and runs along the Namibian border. We pull into an Orange River wine cellar on the road to Upington, only to hear the dreaded hissing of a flattening tire. After the inaugural tire change with the exhaust air jack purchased back in Durban, we wander into the wine cellar hoping the wine will be worth the prolonged stop. The friendly girl who grew up here in the Northern Cape tells us her story of working in Cape Town for a while before returning and marrying a local farmer. They have a farm which runs Dorper sheep, they grow maize and also open the farm up to hunting. Knowing we are from Australia she tells us she has a few Merino sheep. Her father had given her fifteen sheep and over the years she has bred them up to 40 in number. She is very proud of her 'mob' of Merinos. And the wine was worth the stop.

On our first of six nights in the park we camp at *Twee Rivieren* (Twin Rivers) Campsite. There is a restaurant serving game meat which we have tried and enjoyed on previous visits, so we choose the springbok. The meat is tasty and delicious.

Nossob Rest Camp is on the Nossob River which only flows about twice every 100 years but the road is also alongside the riverbed and the wildlife likes the sweeter grass there. We see blue wildebeest, black-backed jackal, gemsbok, springbok and an abundance of birdlife – secretary birds, kori bustards, tawny eagles, goshawks, ostrich and plenty of sociable weavers. The huge communal nests of these weavers hang from large thorn trees and can house up to 300 birds, including chicks. But best of all we see cheetah some distance across the riverbed, but still close enough to watch through the camera lens and the binoculars. There is a fresh kill which we may have just missed, and the two cheetahs are eating what looks like a young gemsbok. For some time we sit there watching their behavior as they feed, the cheetahs taking turns to chase away the jackals which come in quite close. Gemsbok that probably scattered during the chase gradually come back and one young gemsbok reunites with its mother. They stand quite close and watch, knowing there is no longer immediate danger from these cheetahs.

Bitterpan Wilderness Camp, a 4x4 drive across red sand dunes with a beautiful dark storm-cloud backdrop on this day, has four Reed Camps (or chalets made of timber and reeds) overlooking a large salt pan, with wildlife occasionally wandering across. The rooms and communal dining room/kitchen are raised and enclosed by a low fence. On the fridge is a notice: 'Do not spoil what you have by desiring what you have not, but remember what you now have was once among the things only hoped for.' It seems true just now!

We sense a degree of danger as we cook our barbecue over a huge fire in the unenclosed *braii* area which is open to any passing wildlife. Lions are on our minds. With a typical vibrant red African sunset in the background, we share our meal on the open veranda of the enclosed chalet with a couple from Cape Town, a couple from Pretoria and two young French brothers from Fontainebleau, near Paris. Suddenly a whistle pierces the silence of the night. The ranger, who lives in a tiny hut close by is warning us there are lions around the camp and we see the beam of his torch dispersing the darkness and spotlighting a pride of seven, including lionesses and juveniles just outside his hut. We all shine our torches from the safety of our enclosure as they walk around. It feels strangely like reversed roles at the zoo.

5.

Swaziland – border crossings, glassblowers, children and kings

It is our first solo border crossing and we are nervous. They can be harrowing experiences. Our first ever was with Paul and Susan just over a year ago crossing from Zambia into Botswana across the Zambezi River. Paul and Susan were border-wise and unfazed by the chaos and confusion, and we followed in awe as they negotiated their way through the perplexity of an African border crossing.

There are myriads of local people crossing the borders with their possessions carried in suitcases or huge overloaded striped raffia bags. No one tries to maintain any semblance of order and helpful signage is only wished for. Long queues are the norm and it is always hectic and noisy. Vehicles add to the turmoil and trucks are lined up for kilometers waiting in a slow queue for their turn to endure a mountain of time-consuming paperwork. Finally, there are those who make their living in amongst the mayhem, trying to earn money on a daily basis either by exchanging currencies or offering their services as fixers, and they crowd around trying to convince you they are the best for the job. We find it is easier to refuse and manage alone.

★★★

Swaziland, however, opens its border to us without any drama and we drive through rich, irrigated farming country where sugar cane stands tall, occasionally bordered by beautiful flowering bougainvillea. There is a degree of buoyancy to our mood. We are in a new country, stamped effortlessly into our passports, and all is well. Needing some firewood for camping, we pull up at one of the countless neatly constructed stacks of wood on the side of the road, and within minutes we are surrounded by ten shy, smiling, shabbily dressed but beautiful children, all eager to help load the firewood for us and collect the small amount of money due.

In contrast, a busload of school children stops for lunch at Hlane Royal National Park not far from our campsite. They are impeccably dressed in uniforms and well behaved, and the teachers are firm. They are on a school excursion and returning to St Michaels in Manzini, which is a large city only second in size to the capital of Swaziland, Mbabane. The children are polite and excited to be framed in our lens for a photo that their teachers have permitted.

Hlane divides its park into three sections and feels more like an open-plan zoo than a wildlife park. In the lion section, an old sleepy male is barely in the mood to move from the side of the road and our dust as we pass. He flops in the grass a few paces away and shows his contempt with a wide cavernous-mouthed yawn. It is still a buzz to see him so close, regal and superior to the passing world, his mane reflecting the orange glow of the setting sun.

The King Sobhuza II Memorial Park and the National Museum at Lobamba give us a greater insight into the kingdom of Swaziland. King Sobhuza II led the Swazi people to independence in 1968. Much to Brian's intrigue, the king had 70 wives, and over 200 children. In traditional Swazi culture, the king is expected to marry a woman from every clan in order to cement relationships with each part of Swaziland. The practice still exists today in a country with modern day economic and social problems, the most worrying of which is its high HIV infection rate.

After busy Mbabane and on the road towards our campsite at Malolotja Nature Reserve, we visit Ngwenya Glass where local craftsmen and women are employed making products from 100% recycled glass. Up to 1700 items are made each day and they include a range of tableware, drinking glasses, vases, jugs and ornamental African animals. Each piece is handmade and mouth blown and the workings of the factory can be observed from an overhead balcony.

The factory was started in 1979 by Swedish Aid who imported all the machinery and equipment and employed and trained local Swazi people in glassblowing. Two of the most talented were sent over to the Kosta Boda glassworks in Sweden to be trained by some of the leading glassblowers in the world. The factory closed in 1985 but was opened again in 1987 when a South African couple found they could no longer buy glass elephants from Swaziland for their collection. They bought the factory, re-opened and now employ seventy local people, including two of the original Swedish trained glassblowers. The people of Swaziland are encouraged to collect soft drink bottles from all over the country and are paid per kilo for clean glass. School students participate in roadside clean-up campaigns in exchange for building materials and the sponsorship of local soccer teams. From every angle it is an inspiring success story and for the rest of the journey we sip wine from Ngwenya wine glasses with little glass elephants positioned high on the stem. Only one makes it back to Australia and in hindsight we wish we had bought a dozen!

6.

Lesotho – Sani Pass, mountains, snow and ice

Sani Pass is legendary in South Africa as the gateway to the 'roof of Africa' and it reads like something not to be missed. The landscape is rugged over the Drakensberg Mountain wilderness and the pass is a renowned 4x4 challenge with its 9 kilometers of 14 hairpin bends on a steep and narrow gravel road from the South African border post at 1,968 meters up to the official Lesotho border at 2,873 meters. In the middle of winter when we arrive the road can cause even more missed heartbeats with snow and slush but Brian is keen and I steel myself for the ride.

We are both apprehensive as we turn on to the Sani Pass road. Slowly we ascend to the South African border post and we are stamped out of South Africa. The climb becomes steeper towards a crisp, blue sky and an overwhelming landscape, but the pass itself is far more challenging than we anticipate. We know Bruno is equipped for the task, and we are in no hurry, happy to crawl along in low gear using diff locks when the road is steep and gravelly, but dealing with other Sani passers is another matter. Oncoming vehicles include local 'taxis' that speed downhill along with the 4x4 tour operators taking tourists up and back for a day trip. Edging past between the cliff face and a deadly drop is not for the faint-hearted. The road is windy and rocky and unpredictable. As the elevation increases, so too does the cold until ice and snow start to appear, lodged in the rocky slopes. On one of the hairpin bends there is a completely frozen waterfall and mud and slush covers the road. Vehicles have stopped in precarious places for their passengers to take photos, including two vehicle loads of local policemen. We take our photos and watch how the back-log of vehicles all negotiate the bend. It is time to give it a try. To our relief Bruno pulls through without a hitch.

The Lesotho border post is located at the summit and we arrive about 3 pm. It feels wildly satisfying and exciting to have climbed the pass and we are stamped into Lesotho with a smile. Sani Top Chalet boasts the highest pub in Africa, and we are ready for a celebration but it seems practical and sensible to firstly secure ourselves a bed for the night. We are not ready for another freezing camping experience just yet. A 'luxury' thatch-roofed rondavel with an ensuite appeals, though there is no running water because the water pipes have been frozen for three weeks. A bucket of water is positioned next to the toilet and we are informed it can be refilled upon request. But we have made it up the Sani Pass! In our room is a complimentary tiny bottle of Amarula crowned in a tiny Lesotho hat with two tiny glasses either side. Amarula is a liqueur manufactured in South Africa and made from the fruit of the African Marula tree. Apparently elephants adore the fruit, hence the elephant symbol on the bottle's label. We have been told stories, true or untrue, of elephants staggering about after gorging themselves on the fruit, which supposedly ferments in their stomachs and makes them drunk.

We walk over to the highest pub in Africa for a well-earned beer and a chat to similarly minded travelers, followed by a great meal in a cozy log-fire atmosphere. In the pub we meet two young South Africans, here to film a documentary on Sloggett's ice rats which inhabit the grassy slopes. Ice rats are frantic little creatures that are hard to spot as they disappear in a flash down a burrow. Now we understand what we had only glimpsed during the afternoon.

The evening concludes with our nightcap of Amarula. No wonder the elephants love the fruit! The taste is heavenly sweet, not unlike Baileys Irish Cream Liqueur, though the contents of the tiny bottle are not enough to warm us in our freezing rondavel where the cold has had too much of a head start on the little heater we hastily start up. A warm bed is the only solution.

The next morning after a minus 8 degrees Celsius wake-up call, we check out of the Chalet. "Lesotho is not for sissies!" claims the promotional pamphlet on the counter. Temperatures can easily drop to minus 16 degrees Celsius in winter it advises. Despite this poetic warning, we have a great drive through countryside covered with a fine blanket of snow, and very remote with occasional villages perched on the sides of the mountains. It is harsh and unforgiving for the nomadic population, local men on mountain ponies or walking with the traditional but meager-looking blankets draped around their shoulders, herding small numbers of sheep or cattle or goats searching for any exposed tufts of grass. Their children have learnt to run down from their huts yelling out to the passing traffic with their hands out for sweets or money.

As we are to discover throughout Africa, it is a country of many contrasts. We pass a diamond mine beside the road on the way to Maseru as well as a lone ski slope. *Mahlasela* is an Afri-Ski 'resort', operational with one ski lift and a few lodges. That evening we meet a couple from Durban at the New Oxbow Lodge further along the road. 'Lodge' or 'Resort' can be deceiving titles because this is a very modest though comfortable stay. Sally and Vin enjoy a skiing holiday every year on the Afri-Ski slopes. As we enjoy their company over dinner they explain their outlook towards the cities in South Africa. They say Durban is for working, Johannesburg for making money, and Cape Town for living. We found Vin's view of apartheid in South Africa thought provoking. According to Vin, South Africa is the only country that gave a name to white dominant rule, and suffered from the consequences.

We taste our first *Maltabella* porridge next morning which has been a favorite with South African families for many generations. It has a rich flavor of malted grain sorghum and is very different in texture and taste to our Uncle Tobys breakfast oats back home.

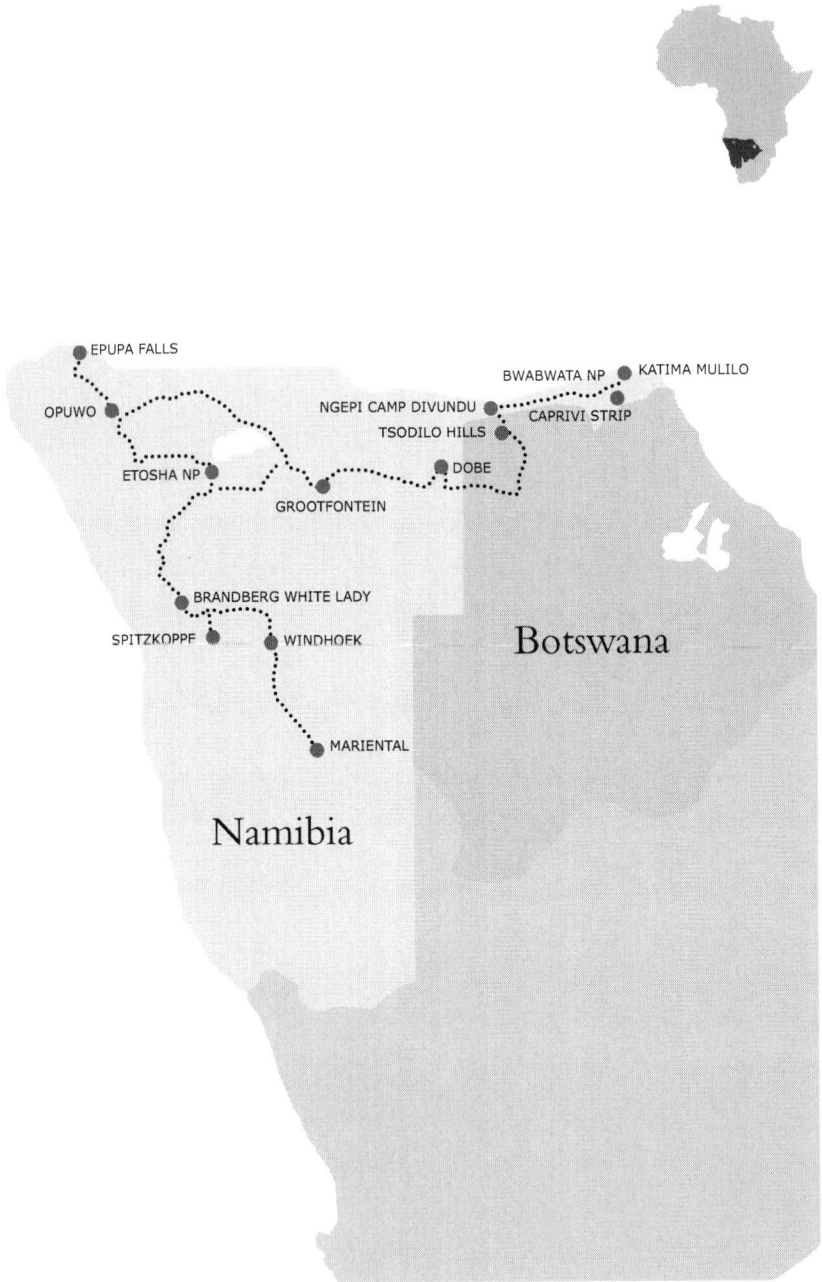

EPUPA FALLS

OPUWO

BWABWATA NP   KATIMA MULILO

NGEPI CAMP DIVUNDU
CAPRIVI STRIP

TSODILO HILLS

ETOSHA NP

DOBE

GROOTFONTEIN

BRANDBERG WHITE LADY

SPITZKOPPE   WINDHOEK

MARIENTAL

Namibia

Botswana

7.

Namibia – giraffe on the run, rock art and tribal tradition

Namibia is a very tourist-friendly country with well maintained straight roads lined with tidy rest areas at precisely predictable intervals, a legacy of German colonization. Near Mariental, we find Koha Guest Farm where our shady campsite within the house yard has its own private facilities and laundry and overlooks the working farm of vineyards, cropping and sheep. Our hostess Johanna cannot do enough for us, supplying free firewood and making sure we are comfortable.

It is here we meet Freddy. After our evening meal we are gazing into our campfire feeling deliciously content and relaxed when Freddy emerges unexpectedly from the surrounding blackness of the night, his startling white teeth contrasting with his black-as-night complexion, giving us an enormous fright. He is the security guard for the farm.

Freddy wanders into our camp smiling and ready for a

friendly chat, with his sparkling smile and eyes to match. He is fascinated that we have come from the other side of the world, and ponders as he gazes at his night sky, just what stars we see back home. Similar to his sky, we tell him, but not so the animals and trees. The landscape and big sky often reminds us of Australia, but the trees here in Africa are nearly all thorny, evolved for protection from hordes of wild animals. Freddy is full of questions about our home, and each answer he repeats slowly, followed by "Mmmm", and then the next question rolls in from his thoughts. Over the next three nights, we become quite attached to Freddy and when he hasn't appeared on the last night, we worry we might not be able to say goodbye. But he does come. He was just delayed by some security 'incident' he tells us, so we are able to give him our farewell gift of a little kangaroo-skin money purse, and we try not to think too much about that 'incident'.

Johanna lets us have a bagful of firewood to take with us when we leave the following morning. Freddy called the firewood *grips* one night after we mentioned how well it burned and how good a campfire it made. At the time we had no idea what he meant but later we realize he was saying *grapes* – the firewood is old grape vines which have been ripped up to be replaced by young vines. After three very relaxing days at Koha we now feel energized to set off for Windhoek and then on to Etosha National Park.

★★★

Along the road to Windhoek we take the obligatory photos of the lonely looking Tropic of Capricorn sign. It feels like a small achievement. Once in the city, at the top of our job list is to organize a car service at the Toyota Dealership. Our vehicle is accepted without even a booking and all the mechanics and staff are so friendly and thoroughly intrigued with our vehicle. They treat it with such reverence and when we return to pick it up, the vehicle is sparkling. They have cleaned every square inch, even the engine looks spotless, and we are waved off like royalty.

Our enquiries about a satellite phone are fruitless. We are given a website and a name and number to call, but the number does not answer. We hope our communication plan works and signals continue to be good as we travel north. This is the case and throughout Africa we are intrigued by the extent of mobile phone use. It appears that landline technology has been skipped or abandoned and every person in the street has a mobile phone. Telco shops and advertisements are in every village, town and city with long queues of customers waiting to top up credit. Some companies have negotiated with owners of little mud brick houses fronting main roads to completely paint the building yellow or bright pink or whichever color signifies their network. Advertising for mobile phones is everywhere. In Rwanda and Uganda we see kilometer after kilometer of trench diggers, local men and women digging meters-deep trenches by hand with hoes, mattocks and shovels for the laying of broadband cables.

The Hotel Pension Uhland is not too far from the center of Windhoek. It is often easier in the cities to stay in reasonably priced little hotels rather than campsites on the fringes. At dinner we sample more African cuisine. Game meat is on most menus and now we have tasted kudu steak, springbok shank, ostrich steak, kudu kebab and springbok pie – springbok is so tender and still the tastiest.

Rule No 3: Never walk or drive at night.

We break this rule for the first time in Windhoek. The owner of our little hotel assures us it is safe to walk to a restaurant. So off we stroll to Lamarmite, a Cameroon restaurant with dishes from all over Africa. In the candlelit atmosphere with ambient African music, we thoroughly enjoy a Cameroonian Curry and a Meat Ragout. The walk home feels a little prickly with few people around even though the streets are well lit, but it is only the next morning when others seem shocked that we walked to a restaurant, that we feel we might have been rather foolhardy breaking one of our rules so flippantly on the recommendation of the hotel proprietor.

Accommodation in Etosha National Park can be booked at the Namibia Wildlife Resorts in Windhoek. We leave with the wonderful prospect of six nights in Etosha – two in a lodge and the other four camping. It's not cheap, but we are in Africa and cannot wait to see more wildlife.

★★★

Spitzkoppe is on the way to Etosha, a spectacular landscape of mountains, boulders and rocks, with photographic colors as the sun sets. Within the community-run campsite is a huge choice of interesting locations to set up camp, all of which are below precarious looking rocks resting on the granite rock face. We survive the night with nothing crashing down – those rocks have possibly been sitting there for centuries weathering away.

Namibia's highest mountain is Brandberg Mountain, a massif of granite in full view of our campsite at the Brandberg White Lady Lodge. On a two hour walk with our local Damara guide Edith, we view some ancient rock art, including the famous

Brandberg White Lady. Discovered early in the twentieth century, the painting is now generally believed to be of Bushman origin dating back at least 2000 years and is assumed to depict some sort of ritual dance, with the 'White Lady' actually a medicine man with his body painted and decorations on his legs and arms. For some time after its discovery, tourists would pour water on the painting to enhance the colors for their photographs which quickly caused fading. The site is now a protected heritage site of Namibia and official guides are compulsory. Edith enlightens the whole experience. On the way up to the rock art she explains the nutritional and medicinal benefits of various native plants and trees. As we gaze at the ancient art form, Edith reveals all its hidden meanings and nuances. That night the locals dance and sing around a fire at the campground, and the atmosphere is mellowed by African voices, so hauntingly rhythmic and uniquely melodic.

Having heard so much about it we are ready to enjoy Etosha. As we drive slowly through the very impressive entrance, our eyes are peeled on the lookout for anything that moves. We see absolutely nothing. But our first stop at Okaukuejo Rest Camp is beyond belief – a picture perfect array of animals wandering around its waterhole, the scene of countless postcards.

It's a treat to drive your own vehicle on 'safari' in an African national park, with the luxury of time on your side, and no pressures to move at any particular pace from sighting to sighting. There are those who dislike Etosha because tourist vehicles career around between waterholes, hoping to give their patrons as much wildlife viewing as possible. They drive in, take photos even with the engine still running, and then race away to the next waterhole. However, with the luxury of time we can sit in our vehicle for hours on end, happy to observe the comings and goings, and the natural behaviors of different animals. We are gazing at the dry, glary landscape striped with magnificent zebras in their prison uniforms one day when our number plate grabs the attention of two Australians. "Are you really from Australia?" The young couple are living and working in the mines in Angola and are on a short hire-drive getaway through the park trying to take advantage of short holiday breaks to see some of Africa.

One afternoon we spot a group of lionesses lolling about not far from one of the quieter waterholes. They are stretched out on their backs, lazing in the sun with a few cubs loitering amongst them. For a long time we sit there just watching the lions, while other vehicles come and go throughout the afternoon. As the sun gets lower, we contemplate returning to camp because the gates are shut at sunset, and not opened again until dawn. The thought of being stuck outside for a night, curled up inside Bruno, is not appealing. Then we notice one of the lionesses is looking intently into the distance and, following the line of her gaze, we spot a lone male giraffe approaching. Giraffes are so very slow coming in to water. They stop continuously to check for predators, before taking a few more paces and checking again. We think the giraffe will be too big to be of interest to these lionesses, but we are wrong. It isn't long before the interest has spread, and one by one the lionesses begin to crouch on their haunches intensely watching the approaching giraffe as he gets closer and closer. Even the little cubs have stopped wandering around and are sitting very still.

We can't leave now! But we are torn and keep checking the downward progress of the sun and trying to calculate exactly how far away we are from the camp, and how long it will take to drive back.

The lionesses are soon in the stalking position, ready to fly. We watch anxiously, half fearful for the giraffe, not even sure we want to witness a kill. Without warning, they are off and away like lightning. The giraffe spots them straight away and scrambles into a retreat. But giraffes are such gangly creatures, and by the time he has wound up some momentum, it looks like it might be too late. His long legs start to pick up pace and rhythm, and although one of the lionesses is literally centimeters from his outstretched tail, he has found his pace, just in time. The lioness soon gives up the chase. Breathing a sigh of relief, we start up the engine and challenge the 50 kilometer per hour speed limit in the park. We race through the gates with the sun and sky a bright orange. What a thrill it has been to see a lion chase in the wild!

★★★

Epupa Falls can be found on the Kunene River in the north-western corner of Namibia which forms the border with Angola. We hear about the falls from other overlanders, who assure us it is definitely worth the detour.

The town of Opuwo is on the way, energy packed with people everywhere, from locals in western clothing as well as westerners, to the traditionally dressed tribal people. The Herero women wear colorful voluminous Victorian style dresses and horn-shaped head gear, reflecting the influence of the wives of German missionaries and colonialists from the early 1900s. Also in the mix are traditionally dressed Himba women. It is a vibrant dusty town, much larger than we foresaw, and perhaps because it is a weekend it seems to rock 24/7 with loud music that we can hear from our campsite – not too noisy but actually quite pleasant. We are high up on a hill above the town in the grounds of the high class Opuwo Country Hotel, where the bar and restaurant, under the thatched roof of the reception area, look north over an infinity swimming pool with 180 degree views of the surrounding valleys and mountains. The campsite itself is a short stroll away and faces west towards more hills and sunsets.

Here we meet a French family, Luis and Nicolette traveling in a hired 4x4 with their three teenage children. A week later we meet them again at Roy's camp north of Grootfontein and we share contact details. Nicolette suggests we visit them in Paris when we drive through Europe on our way back to London. As it turns out we don't as by that stage we are in a hurry to get home and bypass Paris altogether. A few weeks later back home in Tamworth, we receive an email from Nicolette conveying her disappointment so we make a commitment to visit the family in Paris when we return next year.

The Kunene River at Epupa Falls is wide though the flow is controlled by the water release in the dam upstream in Angola. Despite a lower level in the river when we arrive, the falls are still impressive. The river widens around little tropical islands before it plunges through many crevices over the rocks of a geological fault, lined with baobab trees. From a high vantage point on a nearby hill, we notice that the palms and tropical vegetation follow the course of the river on either side for about 30 meters while the surrounding landscape is dry and made up of semi-arid undulating hills. On our last morning the river level has risen substantially, so the water sprays and mists as it tumbles down the rock face, with many more waterfalls than when we first arrived. Our campsite at Omarunga Camp is right on the bank of the river and we are told it is too steep for the crocodiles we see basking in the sun on the other side, which is reassuring. We camp next to a couple from East London, South Africa, who are touring Namibia on two motorbikes with their very young daughter. Wow!

A tour of a Himba village feels intrusive, and we are somewhat uncomfortable but our Himba guide Jason encourages us to take many photos and is keen to give us an insight into the traditional Himba way of life. Proud and friendly, the Himba choose to live in this traditional way even in the twenty-first century. They are a semi-nomadic, pastoral people and breed cattle and goats. The women wear only loin cloths or goat-skin skirts and never bathe, instead covering their skin and hair each morning with *otjize*, a mixture of butter fat and red ochre mixed with naturally perfumed resin which makes their skin appear reddish and shiny, a mark of Himba beauty. They braid and decorate their hair and decorate their bodies with necklaces and anklets. We enter one of the cone-shaped huts made from saplings and bound together with palm leaves, and plastered with mud and cattle dung. Smoke twirls from a goatskin filled with the perfumed twigs of a native tree. The women tend to do most of the physical work, such as carrying water, milking the cows, erecting the huts and caring for children, while the men look after the livestock and are responsible for law and order. The tour includes the cost of some food supplies for the people, as a thank you for our visit, and we buy a souvenir – a Himba 'pillow' carved from wood, only for men mind you, as the women sleep on folded skins or on the arm of their man!

Further up the river is the Kunene River Lodge, a campsite with beautiful native shade trees, full of monkeys, birds and lizards. At the bar on a deck protruding over the water we have a sundowner and watch the sun cast its magic colors through the sky and the reflections dazzling across the river. We chat to a Dutch fellow Paul who has traveled south from the Netherlands! We are excited to meet him and eager for information because he is about to complete the very trip we have started, though he has traveled north to south. He gives us some great travel tips and suggestions of places to visit. Ruaha National Park in Tanzania is one, with a not-to-be-missed meal at the Tandala Tented Camp amongst the elephants and under the stars. We take this advice when we get to Tanzania, as well as his tip for Egypt to travel on the desert track from Luxor to Cairo rather than following the Nile. He assures us it is less touristy and safer and there are great stops at the oases along the way. Paul also gives us the name of his guide through Libya, and enthralls us with his stories of Sudan and how much he enjoyed the people.

Nunda Lodge is situated on the Okavango River on the panhandle of the Okavango Delta near where we cross the border back into Namibia. The owner is from South Africa and spent three years traveling and camping all through Africa, before he and his wife started this new venture. They have tried to use their camping experience to make it a perfect stay for both lodge visitors and campers, incorporating all the features they liked on their own trip. The lodge has a luxurious feel to it with an expansive reception and restaurant area under a thatched roof, and a deck alongside the bar overlooking the river – perfect for sundowners. We try the restaurant, where the local staff members sing a welcome as they play the traditional drums.

Our campsite turns out to be too hot, facing west with glare and little shade from trees that are not yet fully established, so we drive down the few kilometers to Ngepi Camp where the river has twisted around and our camp now faces north east. We chat to Marc, the owner, who is originally from Johannesburg. Marc has been running Ngepi for twenty-one years, having just renewed his lease for another twenty years albeit with some difficulty. Like many nations today, Namibia is trying to restore much of its land to its original indigenous owners. Marc belongs to the Hambukushu Lodge Owners' Association which operates for tourist enterprises in the area and tries to conserve the limited resources, often paying more than the lease agreements to the traditional tribal authority to preserve the local traditions. Indigenous trees are being nurtured and replanted and even the design of boats and engines are being modified to prevent erosion or flooding of nesting birds along the banks. The reeds and grass for walls and thatched roofs are made from local renewable sources in the immediate area, and the treated poles and wooden decks come from commercially grown timber to preserve the surrounding forest habitat. All the rooms use solar power for lighting and hot water, and garbage is separated to be transported to various recycling plants in Southern Africa. Marc tells us jokingly that he cut down the apple tree that was growing there when he first arrived so that he could keep this 'Garden of Eden'.

For those without their own camping gear there are bush huts and tree houses positioned amongst the trees to preserve the natural beauty. The tree houses are self-contained with only one room which is open-sided and surveys the river so that in the morning on waking, as Mark says, "You will have sunrise between your toes". Quirky signs point out the facilities. A 'Loo with a View' is perched up a tall ladder on a platform enclosed by reeds on three sides, allowing a view of the landscape from the 'seat' provided. Other 'thrones' and reed-enclosed showers also have views over the Okavango River. Corny yet funny signs are all over the campsite. 'Please tell reception immediately if you lose your sense of humor' is typical of the feel of the place.

The welcoming sign on the road into the camp reads:
NOTICE
All drivers of 4x4s
Engage 4WD
Select low range
Lock all hubs + diff
Cross your fingers
Everyone else just drive normally!
(Don't worry 4WD is not needed
But it helps them justify the
Cost of buying or hiring one.)

From the comfort of our camp chairs we spend a whole afternoon hippo gazing. The hippos are floating about in the river right in front of us as we sit in relative safety on a steepened bank, once again too steep we are told for them to clamber up on this side. We watch as they climb up the opposite bank for a brief stint of grazing then slide back into the comfort of the river. They are hard to photograph in the water especially in the heat of the afternoon when their heads only surface to take a short breath and by the time you have located them in your lens, they have disappeared. That night there is a full moon and we have roasted a chicken in our camp oven during the afternoon. We eat our roast dinner on the river with the rising moon in one direction, and the colors of the setting sun in the other, and hippos grunting and snorting away in the background. It is not too hard to take!

You can actually swim in the river, in a floating enclosure or river pool suspended by bobbing 44 gallon drums as the river rushes through. It is described by Ngepi Camp as "the world's first hippo and croc cage". We try it, and yes it feels safe from hippos and crocs, but it's not a leisurely wallow in the water.

Brian talks to one of the local staff members at the camp, a handyman and cleaner, who limps around doing odd jobs. He is a huge soccer fan, in fact was a player himself until his playing days were halted by a leg injury, and now he is just coaching. Brian asks the name of the team he played for – the Ngepi All Stars of course! Even the smallest villages throughout Africa have 'soccer fields' often with makeshift goals and an original surface of bare red dirt, or clumps of grass. We often see young children kicking a crude ball made of plastic bags or rags and sometimes just playing soccer in the middle of the road.

★★★

Leaving the panhandle of the Okavango Delta, we stop for groceries at a road junction supermarket. Perhaps there has been a rush on supplies, but there is little on offer and there are shelves and shelves of the same products. At least it doesn't look empty which is often the case in 'supermarkets' in small towns or villages, where footsteps and voices echo, and in the semi-darkness of old timber buildings, the items look lonely on the near-empty shelves. Spar supermarkets are plentiful in southern Africa and no different to a supermarket chain back home. However, there are also supermarkets that are run by Indians and have a completely different feel to them, more of a family-run atmosphere with narrow aisles and towering shelves.

★★★

Before we left Durban, we followed our instincts and filled our store cupboard to the very brim, not really knowing what lay ahead. We now know that a copious supply of ordinary tinned food usually takes up space in the store cupboard for most of the journey. Instead, a good supply of cracker biscuits is essential, with some sort of spread or topping – quick and easy for those times when cooking is too hard or you are just dead tired. Items we learn to do without as we travel further north are milk, yoghurt and butter, primarily because refrigeration in shops is often second rate or non-existent, and frequent electricity blackouts make refrigerated dairy goods risky.

The Caprivi Strip looms ahead. Although we know it is safe to drive through these days, its troubled history leaves a reputation that is hard to shake. This narrow corridor of Namibian land, which has always been of strategic significance, protrudes eastward from the Okavango Region for about 450 kilometers between Botswana in the south, and Angola and Zambia in the north. In 1890, Caprivi was exchanged with the UK for the island of Zanzibar so that Namibia, which was then German South-West Africa, had access to the Zambezi River and a route to Africa's east coast. Military and terrorist incursions have plagued the Caprivi Strip over disputed boundaries. We are heading for Katima Mulilo, the Caprivi Strip's largest settlement, where we can cross the border into Zambia and on to Livingstone and the Victoria Falls.

The Trans-Caprivi Highway is a long stretch of paved road passing through occasional villages with countless roadside 80 kilometer per hour signs. Despite seeing many elephant warnings, the angry and aggressive bull elephant we encounter on entry, and immediately leave behind, is our only view of wildlife migrating through the park. Halfway across the Strip we camp at Bum Hill, one of two community-run campsites in the Bwabwata National Park (formerly Caprivi Game Park). Bum Hill is on the shore of the Kwando River and each bush site has its own 'ensuite' below a three meter platform with a ladder and we haul our chairs up to sit on our private deck and view the landscape listening to and watching the myriads of birds while we sip our sundowner. There are no elephants or hippos in sight, but later as we try to sleep the night noises are deafening, with tinker bell frogs sounding just like wind chimes, and we hear the hippos snorting.

Nambwa Campsite is only 12 kilometers away, across the river and along a sandy 4x4 track. Nambwa is the more remote and quiet of these two community campsites and we camp under a huge shady tree on the river bank after a drive around the park spotting reed buck, kudu, impala and a herd of about twenty elephants around the Horseshoe, a huge loop in the river. At night we see fireflies or glow worms down on the water's edge. We tiptoe closer to make sure, but not for long and retreat to the safety of our camp to tune into another nocturnal concerto.

Along the rough track back to the Trans-Caprivi Highway next morning, we pull up on a hill overlooking the road as it crosses the Kwando River so that we can re-inflate the tires in preparation for driving on a sealed road again. While wandering around we suddenly realize we are at a disused wartime vantage point – spent ammunition shells lie discarded around and a rough cement block with old rusty bolts appears to be a secure point for heavy artillery. It is the only sign we see of past conflicts.

★★★

We leave Namibia at Katima-Muililo and our entry into Zambia at Shesheke is the first of our hectic border crossings. We cannot find immigration or customs, not believing it could possibly be that non-descript building we have already driven past a couple of times. Eventually, we are waved over by a friendly local, relieving us from the frustration of feeling lost, and we embark on the pillar-to-post search for the right office or window for visas, vehicle insurance (this is where we get our Yellow Card insurance which will cover us until Egypt), the unexpected road tax and lastly the unexpected council rates. We pay for visas and insurance with US dollars but the hefty road tax has to be paid in Zambian kwachas of which at this stage we have none. We lose in the conversion rate from US dollars but this is all par for the course on borders where there is a grey area around charges and pocket money for officials and money changers. The council rates are a trick and we are directed to a broken down old caravan where a very disinterested young woman sitting at a rickety table is not pleased to be interrupted while doing the crossword in what looks like a New Idea magazine. The small fee has to be paid in South African rand she tells us, a dual currency with Namibian dollars. I have kept some rand for my souvenir currency collection, so my rand collection shrinks. At last we are through our most involved border so far and we cross the massive new concrete bridge over the mighty Zambezi River.

Little by little we are becoming border savvy and it is here we start to compile our Border-Day Checklist. It evolves over time, and eventually includes: passports and carnet close by and ready, retrieved from their hiding place; the answers to where we have come from and where we are going to (the mind can go completely blank in these situations); the exact location where we will exit the country; how much money we will spend in the country (it is a question frequently asked on forms); and finally we familiarize ourselves with the local currency we will be using, how much it is worth in Australian dollars, and even try to secure a small amount before we enter the country. We avoid exchanging currencies on borders. When we are about to leave a country we use our remaining cash to fill up with fuel.

It is always the vehicle that presents any problems and makes a border crossing more challenging. Our passports create very few queries or hassles with just the usual waiting in queues but the vehicle is a completely different matter. It can often become an opportunity for officials to contemplate making life a little difficult and therefore making a little extra money on the side.

8.

Botswana – ancient hills, spirits and mind games

We cross from Namibia into Botswana at Dobe, a very remote and desolate border post at the end of a rugged road seemingly in the middle of nowhere, in an area still known as Bushmanland and part of the wider Kalahari. The border officials are very relaxed, and we even open one of the boom gates ourselves. We have no cigarettes for the border official on the second gate, but he is pleasant enough.

Botswana is best known for the beauty of its Okavango Delta and its exciting wildlife parks – Moremi, Chobe and the vast and arid Central Kalahari Game Reserve were all highlights of our 2008 trip. But we are drawn back to Botswana to visit the Tsodilo Hills, a mystical and spiritual place of great significance both to the San Bushmen, who periodically inhabited the hills for about 30,000 years, and to the Bantu people who followed during the last millennium.

Both San and Bantu believe the spirits of the dead are

contained in these hills and that powerful gods live in the caves. There are approximately 2000 rock paintings from the thousands of years of human habitation here and it is a UNESCO World Heritage Site. Rising spectacularly to 400 meters out of the hazy and monotonous desert landscape of low shrubs, are two main hills called Male Hill and Female Hill, and two much smaller hills, Child Hill and Grandchild Hill.

We arrive early afternoon and organize a walking tour with a local guide. It is supposedly a two hour circuit around the Female Hill, but it is far more challenging than we had anticipated. Some of the more inaccessible paintings require high climbs with wide views across the landscape, followed by steep rocky descents. The red finger paintings are worth the endeavor. Viewing the images on rock faces across virgin scrub only enhances their ancient aura of intrigue. The rock art on our walk is of animals but reportedly there are also paintings of geometrics and some human figures throughout the hills. The paint is generally believed to be of pigments from ash, plant dyes and various minerals, probably iron oxide in the form of ochre, with binding agents of animal fats and derivatives of plants.

It is quite late when we finish so we decide to stay the night. The facilities at the managed campsite at Main Camp are disappointingly neglected, so we bush camp below the Female Hill at Makoba Woods, with a view to the Male Hill, and we have it all to ourselves.

Is it the lonely site in the night shadow of these sacred San hills? Or is it perhaps the ponderings about ancient beliefs and spirits of the dead that play tricks on the mind? An early night after our strenuous walk and the stillness and quiet is all-embracing, not really conducive to sleep. Sometime during the night we hear a noise in the distance. We think it is a vehicle, but it rolls in closer and louder, and as we lie still in our camper, we realize the leaves are rustling, and the canvas starts to rattle and flap as a gust of wind sweeps over our camp and moves on. The rest of the night continues to be far from sleep-easy with sudden whooshes of blustery wind followed by ghostly silence. Imagination takes over and it feels eerie, mystical and spiritual in the sheer black of a moonless night. We long for the light of day. At last the twitter of morning and we have a reassuring breakfast and watch and listen to the birds around us while the sun rises between Male and Female Hill and warms into another day. It feels special to have experienced a night here on our own – now that it is no longer dark!

Just before we leave two men pull up in their vehicle and have a friendly chat. One is a local chief who is about to show his fellow countryman around this special place. This man has traveled from Gaborone, the capital of Botswana, and is pumped at the prospect of spending the day here on his very first visit. We have only a small hint of how they must feel with their close connection to this landscape. It reminds us of our Aborigines back home in Australia and their strong spiritual connection to country. We are glad we came.

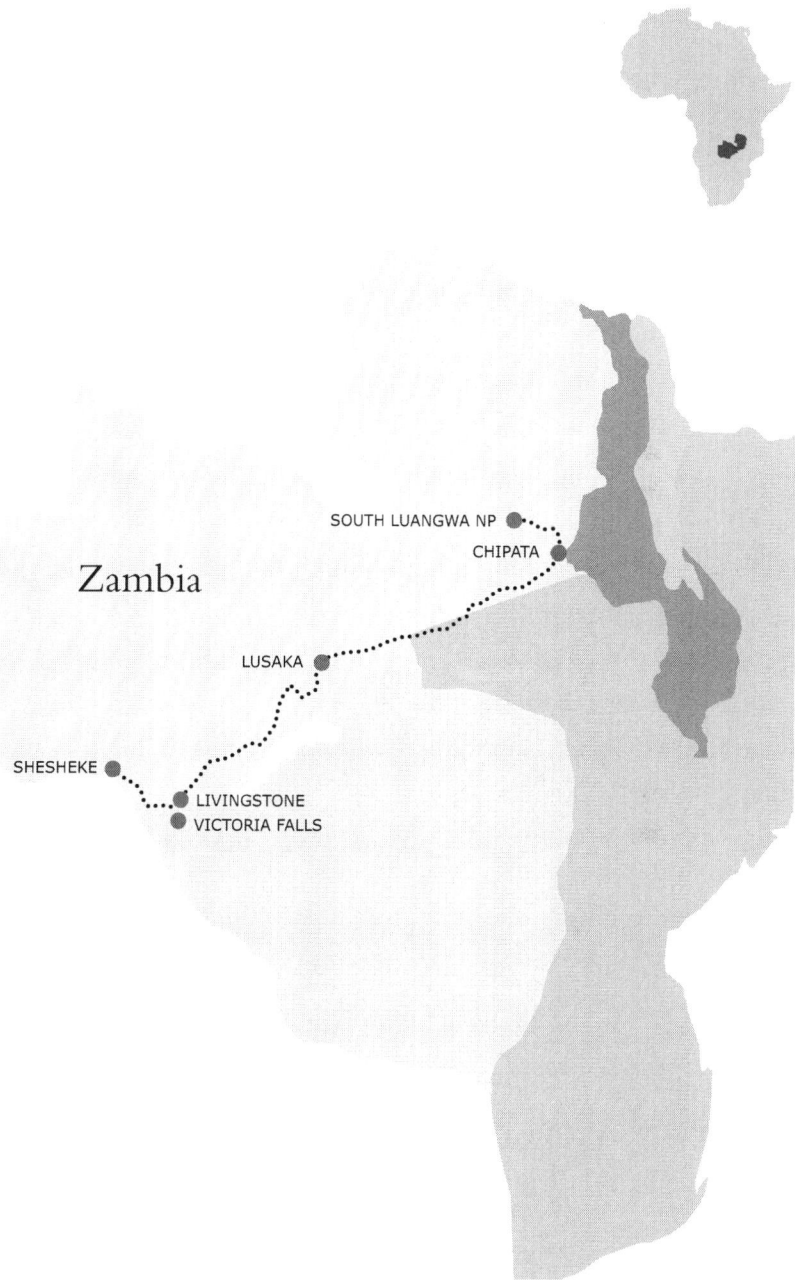

Zambia

SOUTH LUANGWA NP

CHIPATA

LUSAKA

SHESHEKE

LIVINGSTONE
VICTORIA FALLS

9.

Zambia – Victoria Falls, Zambezi River sunsets, local beer and laughing hippos

New currencies are fun and exciting, scrutinizing each coin and its design and getting used to a new calculation for quick conversion to Aussie dollars. In Zambia at this time one Australian dollar converts to about 4,000 Zambian kwachas, so coins are worthless trinkets. A bulging wallet is the norm and millionaire status comes easy – at every ATM.

Victoria Falls is one of those iconic tourist destinations of the world, part of your knowledge base since remembering started. It is neither the highest nor the widest waterfall in the world but it is claimed to be the largest.

We first saw the falls with Paul and Susan at the peak of the flood season last year. The cloud of 'smoke' formed by the massive spray could be seen from the air as we flew into Livingstone, and this prompted us all to blow our budgets and experience the Flight of Angels helicopter ride and see the falls within the perspective of the surrounding gorges revealing its geological history. Such a spectacle was worth the budget scare. Back on the ground as we approached the walking tracks we foolishly declined the offers of cheap plastic raincoats from the locals – a mistake. Luckily, we had a plastic bag for the camera, though at times we could only catch intermittent shots from the viewing points between the surges of mist, spray and teaming water. It was more like a torrential rainstorm than mist and we were totally drenched. It had us screaming with laughter as we negotiated the torrent of water that poured down all the paths. Overall, it was a never to be forgotten experience. Back at the camp we had to peg the soggy contents of our pockets onto a clothes line – wallets, kwacha notes, notebooks and the entry tickets.

This time our visit coincides with the dry season and we have a completely different experience. Instead of the roar and rumbling of an explosive curtain of water plunging over the cliff edge, there are individual rivulets and streams negotiating their way through exposed rocky islets and boulders of dried moss. The two main islands are clearly visible, one of which is Livingstone Island from where David Livingstone first saw the falls in Zambia. We later walk down to the Boiling Pot which is at the base level and the water has formed a pool, but what we see is definitely not the 'boiling pot' it must be in the rainy season. There is a tropical feel to this place with plenty of greenery and palms and a view back up towards the Victoria Falls Bridge linking Zambia and Zimbabwe.

There are people on foot, crossing the lip above the falls so we walk back up the river to find an entry point to try it for ourselves and see how hard it is. We are approached by a guide who offers to show us the way across, which is just as well because the water is traveling faster than it looks to be from a distance, and some of the moss is wet and slippery. Our guide dodges these patches and picks a track on the dry-moss rocks and boulders. It feels weird walking across the path of what can be a devastating torrent of water. I still manage to fall into the Zambezi River, feeling very much a *mzungu* next to our trusty guide who knows exactly where to place his feet and whose helping hand I now accept each time it is offered. *Mzungu* is a Swahili word which is the name given to white people, generally tourists, in Southern and East Africa. Translated literally it means 'aimless wanderer' which well describes how I feel just now.

The Waterfront provides all types of accommodation on the Zambian side of the river near Livingstone, a short distance from the falls. There is a spacious campsite which is very popular with overland trucks and travelers. The bar boasts an expansive view over the Zambezi River and you can hear the roar of the Victoria Falls just a few kilometers down the river. When the sun sets from this vantage point it literally falls into the river as a bright orange fiery ball against the darkening sky. "Just another day in Africa," a guide once said to us on the Okavango Delta in Botswana as we sat in awe of a sunset from a *mokoro*, a small dugout canoe. And here we are again, "Just another day in Africa" chatting to travelers from all over, and sipping a local Mosi beer while the sundowner cruises return to the river bank.

★★★

The name Mosi Lager comes from the indigenous name of the Victoria Falls *Mosi-oa-Tunya*, meaning 'The Smoke that

Thunders', and the falls are depicted on the label. We always try the locally brewed beers – it feels good to support the African breweries rather than stick to the known worldwide brands and it often sparks a smile from the bartenders. The alcoholic content varies widely, but at the end of the day it's just a time to sit and relax and enjoy the atmosphere. Windhoek Lager is the more common beer in Namibia. Not surprisingly Kilimanjaro Lager in Tanzania has a snow-covered image of Africa's highest peak on the label, and it's not long before we realize the request at the bar must be "Two Killis please". Tusker in Kenya has a black elephant silhouette on a yellow background and in Mozambique we try the 2M beer. Ethiopian beers include Harar, Dashen and St George – the latter is a curious name with a logo of a medieval knight, not what you would expect from one of only two African countries which are considered to have never been colonized. Stella Lager Beer (not the Stella Artois that we know back home) is the most popular beer in Egypt but there is also Sakara Gold, and Luxor Weizen which has a label depicting the avenue of ram-headed sphinxes which we see at the Karnak Temple in Luxor, but is terrible beer which tastes too much of hops and has sediment in the bottle. We try Mutzig in Rwanda, and Castle Lager was all the go in South Africa.

★★★

The Mosi-oa-Tunya National Park borders Livingstone and all the attractions and lodges along the Zambezi River near Victoria Falls, so wildlife can occasionally wander into unexpected places. Relaxing at our Waterfront camp one afternoon we spot a herd of elephants feeding right up next to the tall boundary fence and as we watch them at close hand, the Waterfront security guards tell us we will get a much better view if we wander into the lodge next door through a nearby connecting gate. They assure us it will be okay.

The David Livingstone Safari Lodge and Spa is a very upmarket lodge which has only recently opened. Not long after we go through the gate, a very smart looking female security guard confronts us questioningly, but when we explain our mission, she responds, "I'll escort you". She takes us around to where we indicate the elephants should be, and she even gasps in shock when she sees just what the elephants are up to. They are outside the entrance uprooting all the newly planted palms, knocking over large pot plants and totally destroying all the freshly laid turf. After all it is their park, and there is absolutely nothing anyone can do about it. I often wonder whether the lodge ever bothered to restore its grand entrance.

The young security guard then offers us a tour of the lodge, and despite our less than glamorous camping attire we accept. The lodge has a beautiful position right on the river with reception, restaurant and rooms taking full advantage of the view. We put this lodge on our 'lodge-hop' list – lodges that we can dream about visiting on a 'plane-hop' around Africa in twenty years time, when sleeping under canvas might no longer appeal.

★★★

Everywhere in Southern Africa there are locals who scrape together a living by offering to guard vehicles which are parked out in the street unattended by their owners. On returning to the vehicle it is expected that a small fee will be paid. Often the car guard is nowhere to be seen, but the moment the key is in the ignition, he appears at the driver's window. It is a recognized enterprise and in some cities the car guards often wear vests to distinguish themselves as bona fide car guards, and large shopping centers sometimes employ a team of them in their car parks.

In Livingstone we have an unpleasant car guard experience We need to secure our Yellow Card insurance and the building is located in the main street of Livingstone. Every day is a busy day in African towns and cities, always hectic with people crowded along footpaths and crossing the roads weaving in and out of traffic. We manage to find an empty parking space in the main street, and a man offers to watch our vehicle for us. Our car guard is waiting for us when we return and we pay him an amount we believe to be fair, but he is not happy. We understand he wants more money, but we are not sure and are still discussing what we should do, not keen to open our wallet for more money at this stage. A well dressed African man then approaches and tells us politely that we should pay him more. He gives the impression of being helpful and suggests an amount. It seems too much but in the heat of the moment we hand over the money and the man gives it to the car guard. We hop in our car and drive away, happy to distance ourselves from the situation. Reflecting on the incident, we later ask a car guard in a shopping center car park what he considers to be a reasonable amount to pay for a car guard in the main street. We paid five times the amount – not a large sum of money in real terms but we now wonder how much of our payment the car guard received.

★★★

On the road from Livingstone to Lusaka, capital of Zambia, almost immediately we are on a side track. A brand new road is being built by the Japanese and we have a nightmarish 30 kilometer stretch of corrugated gravel road, shrouded in dust from trucks and local traffic. Roads are constructed in ten kilometer sections, and the last section looks complete with a beautiful new surface, but it is not yet open to traffic so we can only imagine a smooth ride as we crunch along in the dust.

We are heading for Chipata near the border with Malawi, and from there a rough road to South Lwangua National Park, and Croc Valley campsite, scene of the elephant and hippo encounters. At Bridge Camp on the way, where the bar and restaurant look across the Luangwa River to Mozambique, an overland truck is already pulled in and travelers have started erecting their tents and are heading for the showers. Suddenly the driver and his offsider are rounding up their charges, telling them this is no longer where they will spend the night. Apparently the campsite owner is not prepared to allow the driver and crew to stay free of charge, so they refuse to camp there, and set off about an hour before sunset, though the next campsite is many hours away.

Anya and Petrus, a South African couple now living in Lusaka, are camped beside us and proudly show us their brand new camper trailer which is on its inaugural camping trip. They are also heading to Croc Valley where we meet them again, but without their brand new trailer camper. On the way the trailer rolled and nearly took the vehicle with it, but luckily they were unharmed, though very shaken. They were only able to salvage the camping fridge, everything else was destroyed. The roads in Africa can be unforgiving.

We stay at Croc Valley for a week, binoculars always at the

ready as well as an escape route back into our camper. The activity on the opposite bank is enthralling. Lions lounge about, luckily unenthusiastic about approaching our side of the river, and crocs sunbake on the many sandy islands. Once we see two local fishermen poling a dugout canoe right past where we saw a huge croc sunning himself on a sand bank just ten minutes earlier. We are quite fearful for the fishermen, especially when they hop out into the shallows to check their nets. Apparently three or four are lost every year − fishermen not nets! Shortly afterwards, back in their canoe, they drift past a herd of hippos without any trouble. Mind you the locals have a great deal of respect for and understanding of the wildlife, more so than many of the tourists who venture way too close. The day we leave Croc Valley, a German couple arrive, and wander away from their vehicle during the unpacking and settling in process, only to look around and see an elephant investigating their open vehicle. "Shoo! Shoo!" they cry, a little foolhardily, but fortunately the elephant decides not to challenge, and saunters away. Admittedly, once we could have easily been fooled into thinking that any animal so bold is less than wild, but we now know they are still very wild despite their show of familiarity.

All week at Croc Valley, hippos once again provide daily entertainment, lolling about in the river, disappearing for a while and surfacing unexpectedly nearby with a snort and their now familiar deep throated "Humm, humm, humm" sound. We camp next to a German couple from Dusseldorf who speak only a little English but manage to good humouredly relate a tale shared with them by their guide in the Okavango Delta. He explained that the hippos tell jokes under the water and have to come to the surface to chuckle at the good ones. "Humm,

humm, humm." For the rest of our journey we chortle along with these underwater comedians.

The Germans generously share one of their meals with us, so to reciprocate we cook them scones in our camp oven, only to learn that he is a pastry cook back in Germany. But he gives the scones a nod of approval, though thinks they need just a touch more salt. We often cook in the camp oven we have brought from Australia, especially when we are staying for more than a couple of nights, and can have a fire. Sometimes we roast a chicken or joint, or have a large meat casserole, but scones are our favorite and fun to share with other campers. Jaques and Mandy, from South Africa, share our scones while they recount some of their experiences driving through Russia and Africa. Likewise, a motorbike rider from England, who has ridden his bike across Europe and south through Africa, tells us stories of his travels.

We meet many Germans along the way. They love the outdoors under the African sky, and it is only a short flight for a holiday, some traveling with their young families. Many own their overland vehicles and park them in various places in Africa, flying back regularly to have another adventure. Another German couple we meet at Croc Valley have quite a large unit on the back of their Toyota, with a huge colored painting of a cheetah on either side. As we admire the artwork, they tell us that many times they have driven into a campsite with monkeys screaming and going berserk, and they are convinced that it is the cheetah on the vehicle scaring them. We don't find it hard to believe because on our last trip to Africa with Paul and Susan, we were camped at Chobe National Park at dusk, having enjoyed our sundowner and had started to prepare a meal. Camping is unfenced in Chobe which can be daunting, and on this evening suddenly the baboons which inhabited the trees around our camp started screaming and jumping around from branch to branch, sounding very panicky. At the same time a lioness was spotted only twenty meters or so away running down towards the water. It certainly added a dimension to our camping and made us super wary for the rest of the night.

Vervet monkeys also warrant a degree of caution. On that same trip with Paul and Susan, we witnessed monkeys snatching food just inches from open mouths at rest stops in Kruger National Park. Another time we were indulging in lunch at an upmarket hotel restaurant on the Zambezi River. A customer's meal was placed before him while he was talking on his mobile phone. Quick as a flash the monkey swooped on the plate and escaped with his loot and it was only after the surrounding commotion of shouting staff pursuing the little bandit and apologizing to the man that he even realized what had happened.

A monkey experience at the Waterfront makes us even more wary of these cheeky scavengers that patrol the campground for a trace of tasty morsels, raiding rubbish bins and even open vehicles. We are walking back from lunch at the bar, and I am watching with intrigue a mother monkey with a baby clinging to her back. Without warning I feel a nip on the back of my leg. Unaware of another female monkey in the other direction, I have walked too close and been perceived as a threat to her baby. She has rushed in to attack and ward off the danger. Thankfully, there was no broken skin which could have been worrying, despite having been vaccinated for Rabies.

From Croc Valley we drive to the Mfuwe International Airport to have a look around and try to post some items. It is a small airport which thrives on the tourism industry, servicing

South Luangwa National Park and other nearby wildlife areas. Driving through the Luangwa Valley the soil is rich, black and the vegetation tropical and dotted with palm trees, banana and mango trees, with many little villages along the way. Stalls sell the local fruit and the usual tomatoes and we also buy eggs, which can be a risk with the uncertainty of their freshness and the diet of the chickens. They are fine and over time we are far more relaxed about buying from these stalls and the local markets. Once we even buy eggs which are sold already cracked open and swilling around in a plastic bag.

On the way back to Croc Valley, we visit Tribal Textiles, a rural enterprise which generates local employment. Local artists design and hand paint cotton fabric and sew it into a huge variety of items such as bed and table linen, wall hangings and home and personal accessories. We join a tour, and watch the process as the first team of craftspeople draw designs on plain calico fabric with flour and water. Paint-mixers play with the colors and create the right shades from three tins each containing a primary color. The painted fabric is spread out and fed through an oven which resembles a moving grill toaster. Once the paint is baked on to the fabric it is washed and the flour scraped away. We are so impressed with the enterprise which exports all over the world, that we cannot resist a souvenir – a vibrant bed throw with an African animal design. Outside are stalls set up by craftsmen who have made little trinkets from wire collected from poachers' traps throughout the park. In Swaziland we saw wire from traps piled high at a park reception, but this is the first time we have seen it used for souvenirs. Poaching continues to be a huge problem across Southern and East Africa.

Mama-Rula's campsite back in Chipata on the border is

run by an extended family of Zimbabweans who have fled from their country due to the uprisings and unrest. They miss their homeland and would love to return some day but in the meantime they have managed to set up this appealing leafy campsite which attracts overland trucks and travelers on their way to the parks in the Luangwa Valley or further north in Zambia. We meet a UK expat, Linda, who has been a guide on an overland truck for over ten years. She is worried about how close they have parked to our camp, but we are not bothered. We are next to a large *braii* area with enough room on the barbecue for the cook to prepare a meal for everyone on board. Linda has a bus full of elderly French couples who are roughing it but loving it by all accounts, erecting two-man tents every night and enjoying the adventure. For Linda this is a dream run, being more used to tour groups of twenty-somethings wanting to party all night who are then a nightmare to get moving in the mornings. Some of the Frenchmen share their whiskey nightcap with Brian before bed, but it is strictly a male-only invitation.

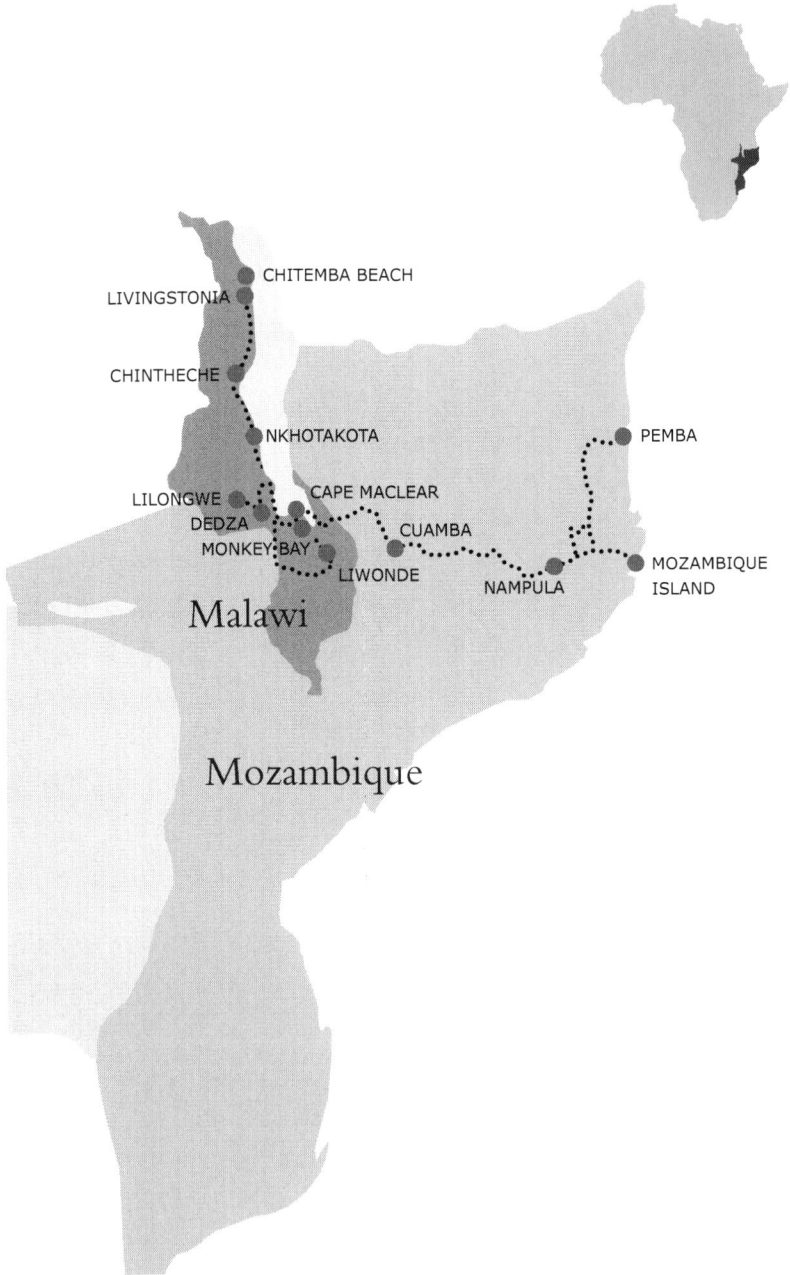

CHITEMBA BEACH

LIVINGSTONIA

CHINTHECHE

NKHOTAKOTA

PEMBA

LILONGWE

CAPE MACLEAR

DEDZA

CUAMBA

MONKEY BAY

LIWONDE

NAMPULA

MOZAMBIQUE ISLAND

Malawi

Mozambique

10.

Malawi – cash only please, lake shores and the start of the Rift Valley

Malawi has rich but over-farmed agricultural land and in recent years government subsidized seed and fertilizer has resulted in an increased yield and some exportation of excess grain. Men and women smile and wave as they carry large hoes with handmade handles to their daily grind on their small patches of land, hand-cultivated in beautiful neat rows ready for the rain, even on the steepest of slopes. Many of the women are hoeing on hillsides with a baby constantly rocking on their backs in a secure little cocoon.

Malawi exists on a cash economy, which tricks us a couple of times. In Lilongwe, the capital, we badly need groceries to re-stock our camper. At the checkout we are embarrassed to find that we don't have sufficient cash to pay for our provisions and they won't accept our credit card so we leave our overflowing trolley behind and dash across to the ATM, returning to hand over our wad of money. The cash is in 500 Malawi Kwacha notes and our bill is 29,930 kwachas. Sixty notes are clumsily counted out on to the counter, then we watch the girl at the checkout recount the money like a professional bank teller, ripping the notes expertly through her fingers at the speed of light – she does get plenty of practice. We leave with a money purse fast filling with small change, and laugh at the thought of paying a three hundred dollar grocery bill back home with five dollar notes.

On another day, we have no idea how much our car service will cost. We have some cash but we are sure a Toyota dealership will take a credit card if we are short. Wrong! We are short and they want cash. There is no ATM nearby and they are reluctant to let us drive our vehicle down to the bank ourselves – in case we don't come back! So a driver takes us to the bank and I sit in the car with the driver, and wonder why Brian is taking so long. I watch him cross the street a couple of times and walk further up the busy pavement. As it happens the first ATM isn't working and then he has to find another and do three transactions because they will only issue 10,000 Malawian kwachas at a time.

Lilongwe is a pleasant city and easy to drive around from our Mabuya Camp, a backpackers lodge and camp site not far from the center. Mozambique visas need to be applied for here. Our plan is to drive across Malawi to Cape Maclear on the southern shore of Lake Malawi, and drive east into Mozambique, across to the coast and up to Pemba before returning again to Malawi and back to Lilongwe. We will then drive north up the lake and cross into Tanzania. This will be the start of a journey through the Rift Valley. Having heard so much about the origins of mankind, we are keen to travel along the western shore of Lake Malawi which is part of the Rift Valley and forms the border with Mozambique.

The Mozambique Embassy is on the outskirts of Lilongwe. It's our first embassy in Africa, and we don't know it at the time, but this is one of the more impressive embassies, an expansive colonial building with the front entrance hall used for visa applications. Later in the journey it amazes us how embassies and consulates send visa applicants to the back door, down alleys, along passageways, up back steps or down the back garden to a pokey room or a line-up at a window. We wonder about the concept that it is unnecessary to try to impress travelers who wish to explore their country. But here in Lilongwe we are impressed, especially when our visas are quick and easy to secure.

A fellow camper at Croc Valley told us about the Dedza Pottery and Lodge which was opened in 1987 and has the largest hand crafted production of pottery in Southern Africa. Dedza is the highest town in Malawi at the foot of Dedza Mountain and on the road to Cape Maclear. We arrive late but not too late to try their famous cheesecake at the Dedza Pottery Coffee Shop, and coffee served in their own distinctive African design coffee cups. Although it seems a rather lonely spot to camp down behind the pottery complex, especially as we are the only campers, we have a pleasant night unworried by the noises of the nearby village which range from children laughing and squealing, to adults talking, laughing and singing, to dogs barking and fighting through the night, and lastly roosters crowing before dawn.

Now the proud owners of two Dedza Pottery coffee mugs, which are in use the whole journey and survive, we reach Monkey Bay, uninspiring with tourists and tour operators so we drive the twenty kilometers further on to tourist-laden Cape Maclear, also known as Chembe. This small fishing village is nestled between tourist venues all hugging the lake. To reach the campsite requires a drive right through the narrow streets of simple clay cottages, forcing people into doorways so that we can swirl the dust around as we drive past. It feels invasive. We see the village at very close hand and the people are friendly but we are not taken by the situation.

We camp at Fat Monkeys Lodge under the shade of three magnificent mango trees (the mangoes are not ripe yet unfortunately) and overlooking the lake. Young boys selling anything to tourists are known as beach boys and stroll along the beach with their wares. They are forbidden to step into any of the tourist venues so they constantly call out to attract attention and entice would-be buyers to look at their trinkets and goods. We walk along the beach where the villagers are washing their cooking pots or clothes which are then draped over the sand to dry. Children are playing on the sand and swimming, men are fishing and unsurprisingly the water looks less than pristine, and the sand on the beach looks very well used. But that's the life of two worlds unfolding around us. Later we sip sundowners as the sun disappears behind Mumbo Island, part of Cape Maclear National Park, where adventure activities for tourists are the drawcard during the day, but where at night the surrounding lights from the local fishing boats sparkle in the distance. It's inevitable that the heightened level of tourism changes these places, and we are tourists and part of the phenomenon, but in some places the intrusion is more pronounced, and this is one of those places.

At Liwonde National Park we are surprised to find so many campers at Myuu Campsite, but discover they are all spending the weekend doing a voluntary wildlife count. In contrast, the next night at the more southern Chinguni Hills campsite still within the park, which overlooks the wide Shire River, we are the only campers. With no one else in sight, we sit and relax looking down on the landscape searching for wildlife in the distance, with a baboon high up in a tree above us eating flowers. Just after our dinner an unexpected visit in the dark from two bare-chested security guards, one with an AK47 slung over his shoulder, initially gives us a massive fright. But they reassure us that we are definitely right for the night under their protection! "Him, him and him," one of the guards says, pointing to himself first, then the other guard, and then his rifle. Very reassuring!

Camped on the shores of Lake Malawi again we meet a South African and his wife. They show us their jiko and we are intrigued. It is a traditional charcoal-burning stove, *jiko* being the Swahili word for stove. An improvement in the design of the traditional jiko was developed in Kenya by local and international agencies and is called the Kenya Ceramic Jiko (KCJ). The KCJ has a ceramic lining in the top half into which is placed the charcoal, with large holes to allow the ashes from the coals to fall and collect in the bottom half. Metal rings flip inwards to allow a pot to sit on the stove. Its hourglass shape directs the stove's heat only to the desired location, right under the cooking pot. Compared to the traditional jiko, the KCJ reduces fuel use as well as emissions of toxic gases and particles. We embark on a jiko-finding mission and it is this search which settles us into the enjoyment of African markets. We eventually find one later in Tanzania.

★★★

An uneasy night awaits further north on the shores of Lake Malawi. We arrive early in the afternoon at Nkwasi Lodge near Chintheche, one of many campsites we have found on Tracks 4 Africa. Our 'Don't drive too far in one day' rule sits well with leaving early in the mornings and therefore reaching our destination around lunch time or shortly after, allowing for a relaxing afternoon reading about our location and looking around, recording where we have just been, or planning where to go next. On the other hand, if our camping destination turns out to be unsuitable, which is usually based on a shared 'gut feeling' and which happens quite often, we still have time to find an alternative.

Driving in from the road we comment that the track looks rather unused as it winds through small crops of cassava, a drought tolerant plant with an edible tuberous root, high in carbohydrate but low in protein and grown all over Malawi. When we arrive it is a picturesque spot right on the lake with little rocky beaches of white sand amongst the jagged rocky outcrops along the shore. The wind is whipping up a small 'surf' and we pick a grassy spot under a huge mango tree. We check in with a member of staff and notice on the register that no-one has stayed there for ten days or so and we are informed that Jim, the owner, is watching TV. However, no 'gut feeling' emerges for either of us and we spend a pleasant afternoon relaxing. No other campers arrive, but we feel safe even though we are a hundred meters or so from the main complex and facilities. We are just about to enjoy a sundowner when a worker wanders over and says that Jim would like us to join him for a drink.

Jim is a grey-haired, unwell looking man and he informs us he has Multiple Sclerosis. He is very thin and gets about on crutches, yet constantly drinks and smokes He was born in Northern Rhodesia (now Zambia), and he has owned the place for twenty years but he seems jaded, speaking scathingly about Malawi and the local people. We had noticed that the place was looking rather rundown, and now it becomes clear he doesn't have his heart in the business any more, having separated from his wife. His workers run the day-to-day business of the campsite, though he shows them no respect while we sit having our beers on the deck overlooking the lake, talking to them rudely, or talking about them while they are within earshot.

It is quite dark by the time we wander back to our camp. We have a fire going which we started up during the afternoon and we roast some cashews we bought along the road during the day. We then proceed to cook our meal in the camp oven. We notice one of the staff members, who must be acting as a security guard, lurking in the background beyond the light of the fire watching us. Brian tries to engage him in conversation but he moves away. Meanwhile a camp dog has taken a liking to us, or perhaps to our meal cooking on the campfire, and we are pleased to have the dog around us. We wonder if the guard is hungry, but when we try to talk to him, he moves away further into the darkness. It is unnerving to have him hovering around and yet unwilling to come closer.

We move into our camper and retire early, but we hear him all through the night and see him wandering around the camp, quite close to the camper. The dog even barks at him a couple of times. It is all very unsettling and we have a sleepless night waiting for the morning. The man is not around when we get up at first light, but our friend the dog is still there. When we arrived the previous day we had thought we might spend a couple of days there as it was a great setting, but we move on early after that one sleepless night.

★★★

The rest of our time in Malawi is spent moving from one campsite to the next on the shores of Lake Malawi, which becomes more remote and appealing as we travel further north. We call in at Nkhotakota Pottery, an enterprise run in conjunction with Dedza Pottery, and where two and three week pottery courses are conducted by the local people with lodge accommodation or camping available. After looking around the workshop we just enjoy a coffee and homemade coconut tart at the café and ponder the fate of shiploads of slaves who journeyed from this point on the lake to frightening, unknown destinations. This used to be one of the busiest slave-trading centers of the nineteenth century.

The Viphya Mountains are a cool respite from the hot and humid climate on the lakeshore. We drive through the largest man-made forest in Africa, a great deal of which has been logged and not replanted, to reach Luawa Forest Lodge, recommended by a local for a different perspective of Malawi away from the lake. The owner left England many years ago to settle in Malawi and we enjoy our chat with him. He has owned the lease for his tourist venture for ten years, and has just been able to renew it for another twenty. Originally from Yorkshire, he initially came to Malawi as a teacher. His ecotourism lodge offers wilderness activities or just peace and quiet in highland plateau woodland. Camped with us are a Dutch couple and their young daughter who are living and working in Malawi. We cross paths with them a number of times over the next week, lastly in Zanzibar where they are attending a family wedding.

Livingstonia was named in honor of Dr Livingstone by Dr Robert Laws who moved the Scottish Missionary there, way up on top of the Rift Valley escarpment to escape the mosquitoes and malaria. The 16 kilometer road up to Livingstonia climbs over 700 meters in altitude along a series of 20 hairpin bends. Except for some concrete that has been put down over the most serious bends, it is a gravel road and the local people have worn paths straight up crossing each bend. It's quite a challenging road, but we get a great perspective from up there of the lake within the Rift Valley. We also call in to the Mushroom Farm, perched up on the escarpment with more amazing views, and run by another Australian.

At Chitimba Beach we have plenty of company in the way of overland trucks and the drivers tell us about 'The Farmhouse' in Tanzania, one of their favorite campsites. We leave Malawi, highly populated and very poor, but with such friendly people who never fail to smile and return our waves.

11.

Mozambique – remote countryside, beaches, 'exotic places' and broken rules

Our Mozambique escapade is a detour during our drive through Malawi. After crossing the border, the long red dirt road across Mozambique is rough and remote with few villages and mostly edged with rich soil growing cashew nut and mango trees and bananas, interspersed with patches of poor scrub. The landscape is constantly dotted with basalt outcrops and rocky hills. Few vehicles use the road, but people walk, cycle or carry loads. Every woman of child bearing age seems to have a baby wrapped up on her back, tiny infants with little sleeping heads poking out or pre-toddlers with little legs and arms dangling and little heads bobbing and sometimes peering about. They always look content and comfortable, though for the mothers who sometimes have a load on their heads as well, it must be hard work. Since Namibia the women in rural areas have been wearing a *chitenge*, a wrap of bright colored fabric often as a covering to keep their clothes clean but also used as a head scarf or a sling for wrapping babies.

We have slipped into the habit of waving to everyone as we drive along, which can become quite a busy pastime, but here we find the people less inclined to wave or even smile and are more intent on their daily living. Life seems hard and impoverished here in the countryside of Mozambique. We notice political flags flying at many of the villages and people carrying corresponding promotional 'sample bags'. Occasional cars full of supporters race past and we work out the two opposing political parties. Elections in Mozambique are not far away.

We know that we can only drive as far as Cuamba on this first day as the next possible night stop is many hours further on. Upon our arrival early afternoon we immediately have the uncomfortable feeling that there will not be too many choices when it comes to accommodation. The hotel mentioned in the guidebook as the nearest thing to an international hotel in Cuamba is not even close, so we drive around looking at the other options, all of which are worse. It seems everyone speaks only Portuguese until thankfully, while getting cash at the ATM, we come across a local who speaks English. After commenting, "Do you really want to stay here?" he suggests we try the Sao Miguel Restaurant and Bar which has accommodation, and which we have already driven past and dismissed as an option.

Back at the Sao Miguel, after various attempts at communication, we are led around the back to the senora who speaks English. The accommodation looks somewhat ordinary, so we ask if we can spend the night in our camper in the very cramped area just outside the rooms. All is now in place for an interesting night. We spend some time slowly sipping coke and eating hot chips in the restaurant, then 'relaxing' in our chairs in the shade of the camper in the thick of the comings and goings around the establishment, and feeling we are a rather unusual sight in these parts. The dogs befriend us and take up residence in our limited space, until we go back to the restaurant for a beer and something else to eat. The chicken is not too bad. Afterwards, as we retire for a very early night, Brian repeats his frequent quote, "I take you to some exotic places!" We drift off to sleep to the backdrop of electioneering cars hooting down the street, lots of shouting and noise, and thunderous booming dance music from two competing venues very close by. Finally, of course, the dogs and roosters herald the morning but in actual fact, through all this, we feel quite secure and do get some sleep.

Another long day of driving and we explore Nampula looking for a possible camping option or guest house. Nampula is rundown, messy, crumbling, ramshackle and full of people and mad drivers, with mini-buses constantly stopping unexpectedly to pick up or deposit passengers. The Portuguese arrived in Mozambique in the fifteenth century after dislodging the Arab sultan from Mozambique Island. The Portuguese influence is clearly visible in the architecture and road building in the towns, with wide streets and median strips and large ostentatious but crumbling buildings in total disrepair. Little has been done to maintain roads and buildings and much has been destroyed since Independence in 1975 followed by a civil war from 1976 until 1992. Such a history is reflected in the people.

No accommodation options appeal during our exploration of the city of Nampula so we retreat to the camping sign back along the road about eighteen kilometers, which didn't appeal at the time, but now seems a possibility. Down a nondescript road we find a campsite situated on a picturesque man-made lake and a security guard carrying a gun. Whether that is a good or bad sign we don't know, but our choices are limited so we set up camp as we watch local families picnicking and enjoying the afternoon. The families pack up and drive away and we realize we are the only ones left camping. Before we finish dinner a carload of late night picnickers arrives, young people ready for a party in the large gazebo adjacent to our chosen campsite. Another night of roaring music to match the previous night in Cuamba, though this party ends before the wee hours. Africans love their music loud!

The tarred coastal road north to Pemba is pulsing with human activity. Young boys sit beside the road with containers of cashews, men and children hold flapping chickens or roosters by the legs, trying to wave vehicles down to make a sale. Anything is for sale – low thatched beds for sitting or sleeping, timber bed-frames, intricately carved doors, fabrics, and always tomatoes. We see a whole family walking along loaded with water on their heads, the children's containers matching their size. As soon as children can walk, they can help. Brick making is common with homemade kilns and hundreds of bricks drying out in the sun. We cross a long, high bridge where a river empties into the sea, and crowds of people are way below swimming and washing clothes in the water trickling by, the colorful laundry spread flat on the rocks in the sun or blowing dry in shrubs.

We have heard that Russell, who is Australian, runs a very comfortable campsite and backpacker accommodation at Wimbe Beach in Pemba. In fact, so comfortable is Russell's Place that we stay for three nights, mostly relaxing in our camper under perfect shade, or enjoying the food and drinks at the restaurant and bar under the cool thatched roof, chatting to other travelers and to Russell who is a wealth of information. He has been in Mozambique for ten years having come from the Sunshine Coast in Queensland. We walk along the beach, idle and unspoiled, the water aqua blue and the sand white, with primitive sailing boats moored offshore. We even have a couple of swims in the Indian Ocean. The tides are huge and at low tide we must wade through shallows for a few hundred meters to find water deep enough for a swim. We explore the town and peninsula, but the previous three long days of driving have taken their toll and it is good to simply relax. Russell's showers are a treat —one large bin sitting on a small charcoal heater, another full of cold water. With saucepans or long-handled pitchers for mixing the hot with cold, the water is poured over the head. Does the job!

It is here at Russell's that we first meet Dickie and Claire and their two young daughters. After spending a couple of years living and working in South Africa, they are now driving home to England, home-schooling their children all the way. They have already seen much of Malawi and plan to drive further north and test the river crossing to reach Tanzania. We chat about the advantages of traveling together later in northern Kenya, Ethiopia, Sudan and into Egypt, and exchange contact details before going our separate ways.

We backtrack down the coast to *Ilha do Mocambique* (Mozambique Island), historically a major Arab port, and later inhabited by the Portuguese who traded gold, ivory, spices and slaves. It is linked to the mainland by a 1.5 kilometer single-lane bridge, just wide enough for a vehicle. All the way across the bridge are little alcoves extending out above the water to pull into if a vehicle comes the other way – a fitting introduction to this fascinating and unique small coral island, three kilometers long and half a kilometer wide.

Mozambique Island is a living testimony of the meeting of cultures, a mixture of African, Arab and Indian cultural elements, known today as Swahili. The arrival of Portuguese traders added more to this cultural mix. Most of the population lives in the Macuti (Reed Town), a tumbledown collection of African settlements erected from natural materials such as thatch. We walk around the Stone Town, where the architectural character was created over a period of 400 years with a mix of colonial Portuguese and Islamic influences on the stone buildings, which today stand with peeling paint and crumbling walls.

Unfortunately, the sixteenth century fortress of Sao Sebastiao is closed for renovations, but we organize a guide and visit the seventeenth century former Jesuit College of Sao Paulo, which was also the governor's palace before it became a museum, along with the Sacred Art Museum. Our accommodation, the Escondidinho, is an old converted Portuguese mansion with a garden courtyard and glimpses of the ocean. Our room is large and painted white with high ceilings and matching white curtains that balloon gently in the cool ocean breeze.

★★★

Our rules, our rules: 1) Don't drive too far in one day; 2) Cross borders in the mornings, not in the afternoons; 3) Never walk or drive at night. We break all three in one day in Mozambique on our way back to Malawi.

We head back to Cuamba, knowing we definitely do not want to stay there again. The experience is one we will remember but one we are not keen to repeat. We want to cross the border back into Malawi further south than where we entered, so we plan to drive straight through Cuamba, take a different road to the border and then spend the night in Liwonde National Park back in Malawi. It seems reasonable and doable when we make the decision, but although we expect a big day of driving, it takes 6½ hours to reach Cuamba. When we leave there at 1.30 pm we feel it is all still possible, but the road deteriorates and the countryside becomes more remote. We notice children either running away or crying when they see our vehicle making its way along the track which sometimes even takes us through their villages, and most of the locals look at us wide eyed as we wave our customary wave. It takes another 2¼ hours to travel the 68 kilometers to the border, which we discover is a bit of an outpost. The border crossing takes longer than it should – it is so small we miss the passport control and customs completely and arrive at the border boom gate with nothing stamped or signed. The official sends us back the couple of kilometers to search for the appropriate buildings or rather sheds, and the appropriate officials.

Once through the border the road gets even worse. As the sun sets we check the guide book for accommodation options in Liwonde as we know we will not make the national park before the gates close for the night.

Still traveling on the road to Liwonde it is now dark and we have to drive very slowly to avoid donkeys, cattle, and people walking or on bikes, or mini-taxis careering through everyone and everything at great speed. By the time we arrive in Liwonde, any accommodation will suit, which is just as well because the campsite on the Shire River is pretty ordinary, and is in the middle of a blackout. In the gloom of the car park, the security guard approaches us and we follow him to the open air bar overlooking the river, all still in darkness. We have a meal at the bar once the lights are back on after setting up camp, once again in a car park – but secure! We spend another night in one of those '...exotic places' after our day of broken rules.

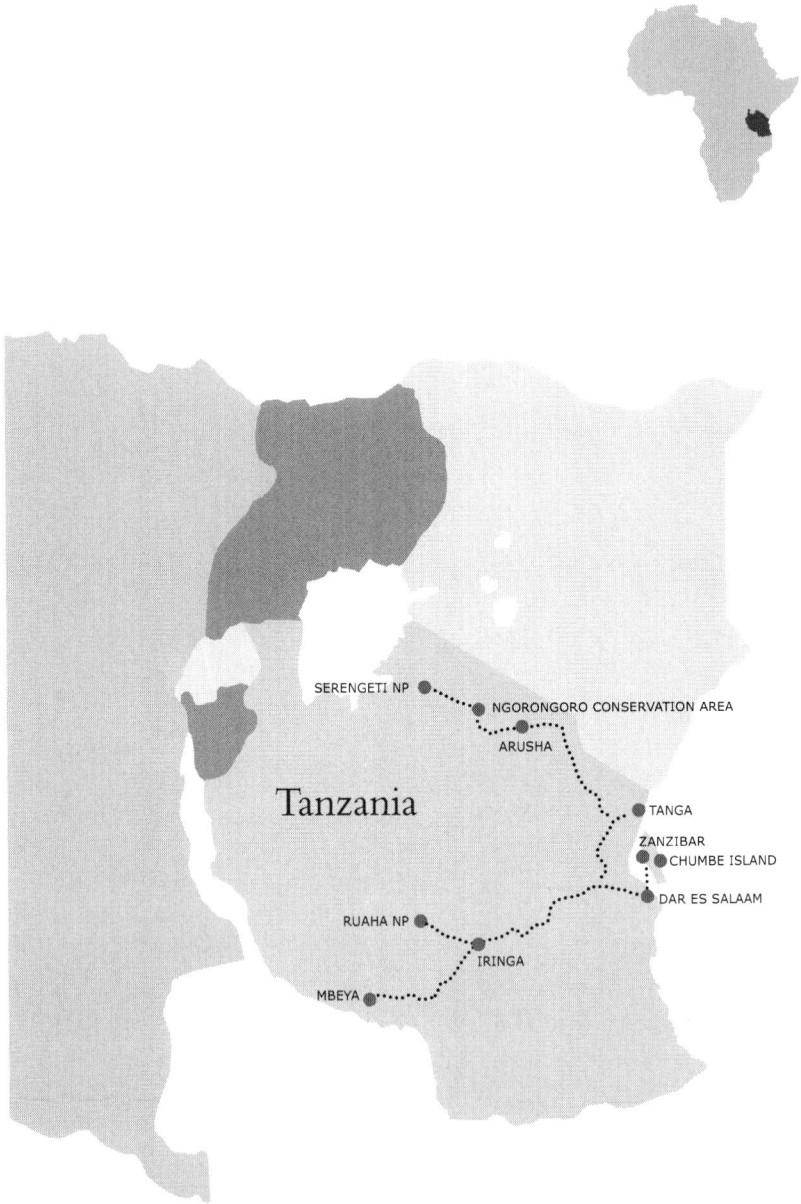

12.

Tanzania – crazy drivers, Zanzibar spices, big cats galore and a wildebeest migration

People are everywhere in Africa. Women and children walk along the road carrying containers of water balanced on their heads, up to twenty liters at a time back to their huts, sometimes many kilometers from the water supply. Children carry younger toddlers and walk to school and back at all hours of the day. Men ride bicycles loaded to exhaustion with thatching for roofs, firewood, charcoal or bags of mealie all piled perilously high, forming a cover over the rider, loads so huge they can hardly steady them surrounded and enclosed in their little space as they strain on the pedals. Goats and pigs are transported in baskets on the front, and pushbikes can carry as many as three adults and a child, all perched precariously on handlebars or racks with the little children safely in front in between the rider's arms. Bakkies, small pick-up trucks, are overloaded to the hilt with people squashed into every corner, limbs hanging over the edges, but thankful to have a lift to work or into town. But more than anything it is the vision of people walking, walking, walking.

Sweeping is a daily activity. Women outside their huts sweep with long straw brooms, keeping the whole enclosure around several huts immaculately tidy, and the pseudo lawns around campsites and rondavels are swept daily. Men work by the roadside, exposed to the sun and glaring heat, smashing rocks with hammers in order to break them up into gravel for the roads.

As we pass through towns and villages, the roads are lined with abandoned-looking buildings of corrugated iron or mud brick. Most are derelict with outdoor stalls in front set up in the traditional African way of selling produce in the street. Other derelict buildings still trade as shops and inside they are dark and dingy as you peer through the gloom at an assortment of goods on the scant shelves. We sometimes see handcrafted Coca Cola signs to lure customers inside to purchase the warm bottles, but Coca Cola is another story in itself in many of the countries in Southern and East Africa. No matter how tiny the village there is a shop with crates of used Coca Cola bottles sitting out the front collecting dust from the passing traffic, waiting for the Coca Cola trucks which traverse the country to pick up the empties and deliver refilled bottles. This is one of the rare examples of recycling we see in our travels in Africa. Pepsi dominates in far fewer locations.

Tomatoes and onions become a staple in our diet, and in most places we have no trouble buying vegetables. In Australia we rarely shop at open markets, but in Africa we gradually begin to enjoy the colorful, mad buzz of the marketplaces. Initially we find them overwhelming and confronting. We feel so conspicuous and lack confidence in negotiating prices. Over time we become more relaxed and enjoy the whole experience. The markets we love are the everyday markets selling food, utensils and clothing to local people. The touristy markets where aggressive vendors sell souvenirs are far less appealing.

Vendors' stalls can line roadsides for kilometers and they all sell exactly the same merchandise, always tomatoes and onions, but also fruit, depending on the season. The produce is stacked in neat and precariously balanced triangles and each stall is attended by at least one person, sitting all day waiting for passing traffic to stop. How must it feel to be one of so many waiting for a vehicle to choose your stall and not the one just a few meters further on? Countless stalls of intricately carved wooden artifacts are also a feature along the roads.

★★★

The Southern Highlands of Tanzania present a hilly, lush-green tropical landscape of rich volcanic soil covered with tea plantations and bananas. It feels energized and people seem busy and industrious managing the produce in roadside stalls or loading trucks. Here we see mechanized farm equipment in contrast to the manual labor seen in many countries so far. Thatched roofs now sit on walls of larger cement bricks, though there is still a proliferation of unfinished or abandoned dwellings and walls constructed around empty blocks of land, which is something we also saw in Malawi.

Mbeya is our first city in Tanzania, busy and bustling and where our first "Jambo!" is beamed to us from a friendly local. *Jambo* is the Swahili word for hello and features in an internationally known Kenyan pop song, Jambo Bwana, first released in 1982 by a Kenyan band called Them Mushrooms. Now there are a myriad of versions and the song is blasted anywhere there are tourists. We hear the tune first in Zanzibar and cannot resist buying a CD. It becomes a compelling sing-along reminder of this part of Africa, and *jambo* becomes our regular greeting to all and sundry from here to Kenya.

Utengule Coffee Lodge is an impressive complex with lodge accommodation and a restaurant looking out over a pool and tennis court and the coffee plantation beyond. We camp within the complex and the Dutch couple Arch and Loes and their daughter whom we met at Luwana Forest Lodge become our camping companions once again. The Utengule Coffee Estate is a large coffee plantation down a dirt road eight kilometers out of Mbeya. Rift Valley Coffee espressos are a feature of our stay here and we stock up on a fairly large tin of freshly ground coffee beans for the road ahead.

★★★

We drive through poor country dotted with forests and occasional swamps and five police checks before arriving at Iringa where we visit a huge market. We are still searching for a jiko. Brian comments on how well we are blending in with all the activity. I'm not so sure about the blending, but certainly no one bothers us or particularly looks our way, all too intent on the task at hand.

Under the cover of a corrugated iron roof there is a food area with all manner of vegetables and we watch a man shelling peas onto a growing pea mound beside him. Aisles of smoked fish, bags of grain, and a never ending list of produce of every sort greet us and we wander further on down the lanes packed with people dodging in and out of honking cars and trucks and barrows. We find clothing hanging from doorways outside little 'shops' where women are dressed in the same beautiful clothing of brightly colored fabric that they are sewing furiously on old treadle Singer sewing machines. Women in Southern and East Africa often dress in beautiful colorful fabrics, frequently with a baby wrapped in matching cloth bouncing along on their backs.

We come to the open air hardware section and there they are – rows of jikos of all different sizes, some of bright shiny tin and others blackened. Which one will we choose? We decide on a black one, thinking the silver look won't last anyway. Throughout the rest of the journey we use it constantly and it becomes battered and bruised from the weather and dusty rough roads. Charcoal is a widely used energy source and is always available by the side of the road, often in quantities far too large for our needs.

In South Africa on our last trip we bought a 'potjie' (pronounced 'poy-key') – *'potjie kos'* is 'pot food'. They are cast iron pots and we chose one on legs with a handle, and took it home in our luggage which was overweight but our potjie arrived home safely. It didn't survive the cull for this trip, beaten by the camp oven which is bigger, and can cook scones.

Not far from Iringa, the Old Farm House, also called Kisolanza, is a working farm run by an English expat. He provides a well-equipped campsite but also the welcome addition of a candlelit restaurant, with beautiful meals using all home-grown vegetables and meat. The surprises that await you as you travel through Africa! Leek soup followed by rump steak, herbed potatoes and vegetables with a dessert of apple cake is not a meal we anticipated at a campsite in western Tanzania. It is here we meet Liz and Peter from England. After hearing their story of traveling from England down through the west coast countries of Africa, no less, through Nigeria, Angola, and both the Congos, we feel utterly pedestrian. And now they are on their way north traveling back to England. They will later become our traveling companions through Kenya, Ethiopia and Sudan.

★★★

Ruaha National Park was recommended to us by Paul the Dutchman back at Kunene River in Namibia. After the 120 kilometer vehicle-shattering rough road, we call into Tandala Tented Camp just outside the park boundary. Accommodation here is beyond our budget, but John, the owner, is more than happy for us just to have dinner there that evening and even suggests we should camp at Chogela Campsite a short distance back down the road. Liz and Peter are staying at a different campsite but we arrange to meet them for dinner at the Tandala restaurant just before sunset, when elephants descend each evening on a waterhole nearby. Two traditionally dressed Maasai security guards greet us at the car park and show us the way while on the lookout for any wild animals. We spot the elephants from the safety of the open veranda bar in the lodge while we enjoy our sundowner and we have an excellent meal at the tables set up under the stars of an African night. We are starting to think Tanzania is a country in Africa not to be missed.

At the campsite we have our second tire puncture. We wake one morning to find we have a vehicle that is going nowhere. Within minutes of entering tire-changing mode, out of nowhere appears Njimi, one of the workers at the campsite, an odd job man about the place. He has come over to lend a hand, but more than anything he is excited. He is laughing and incredulous that we have so much equipment for changing a tire – built-in air compressor, exhaust air jack, and a ratchet for the wheel nuts which works from the 12 volt cigarette lighter. He wants to help at every step, racing to be the first to pick up the tool, or secure an attachment, or let the air out of the exhaust. He enjoys every minute. His enthusiasm knows no bounds, even when it turns out to be a lengthy exercise changing all the tires around, putting the two brand new spare tires on the front. Not only do we have our second puncture in a campsite rather than out on the open road, but we have Njimi, who speaks only Swahili, but makes the whole exercise a treat for us all.

Ruaha National Park is worth the rough drive, the shocking road, and the flat tire. The typically African landscape is dissected by the Great Ruaha River as it makes its way through the savannah grassland dotted with majestic trees, including baobab trees and the classic umbrella thorn acacia. We have a 24-hour game viewing pass in the park, and on the morning drive we suddenly see there in front of us, so close, so relaxed, a pride of lions. There are about ten lionesses and a few young ones lounging about under a tree during the heat of the day. We sit there for quite some time in the safety of our vehicle, just enjoying the spectacle. Inaccessibility has insured this park has remained virtually unchanged for centuries, and even today there are fewer tourists than in many of the other parks.

★★★

We have two near misses within half an hour on the road

to Dar Es Salaam. Roadwork is in progress and vehicles are forced on to a dusty side track. A truck is approaching with dust billowing behind, when suddenly just as we are about to pass, a vehicle appears out of the dust on our side of the road begging for a head-on collision. There is little time to correct for either of us, but miraculously we pass without incident and are grateful we are driving slowly. Shortly afterwards, climbing a hill and negotiating a bend, we are face to face with a loaded bus overtaking a truck rather too fast down the hill. We have nowhere to go with a steep drop to the side, but the bus averts a collision, squeezing back in where it belongs. Drivers here have no need for defensive driving courses that are available back home – they just practise every day in this part of the world.

Dar Es Salaam is not the capital but is Tanzania's primary city, important for business, government, education and transport for the whole of Tanzania, and the traffic is scarily chaotic. Our Mikadi Beach Resort campsite is south of Dar Es Salaam, a five minute journey from the city center across its natural harbor on the Kigamboni Ferry, which carries both passengers and cars. But our GPS initially takes us the long way round on a forty minute drive which avoids the ferry and more city traffic. We later learn that it is the less stressful way when driving a vehicle.

Mikadi Beach Resort is run by a young married couple, Jo from Zimbabwe and Lucho from Chile. It caters very well for overland travelers, with *bandas* or thatched raised huts for those without camping gear. It is situated right on the beach, and is pleasant and friendly with good food at the bar/restaurant, and constantly patrolled by Maasai security guards. While we are setting up camp, we notice some vehicles parked close by and presume that the owners are over in Zanzibar, as we know it is possible to leave vehicles parked at the campsite. It isn't long before they all return from Zanzibar and suddenly we are included in a campsite of ten people, as we have inadvertently plonked ourselves right in the middle of the best camping area. And unbelievably, one of the vehicles belongs to Dickie and Claire and the girls whom we last saw at Russell's Place in Pemba, Mozambique.

We explore Dar Es Salaam on foot, catching a *bajaj* (a small three-wheeled Indian vehicle) from Mikadi Beach to the Kigamboni Ferry and then joining the masses commuting to the city. The ferry is quite an experience, noisy and hectic, with queues of passengers and vehicles lining up in organized chaos waiting for the rush to board. Another day, Bruno braves the ferry for a drive to Msasani Peninsula north of the city, home to many expats whose accommodation is provided as part of their work contract. Most houses are spacious two-storey villas or bungalows on gated blocks of land. We visit the Slipway shopping center, very upmarket with an art gallery and serviced apartments, but a world away from the city just a few kilometers to the south. It is 7.30 pm and already dark when we catch the ferry back to Mikadi (Rule No 3 broken again!)

★★★

Chumbe Island has been highly recommended to us by Paul and Susan. Chumbe Island Coral Park lies between Zanzibar Island and Dar Es Salaam, and can only be reached by boat from Zanzibar. At the Zanzibar ferry terminal we meet a couple from Sydney and he has returned to Dar Es Salaam where he lived until the age of twelve, his father employed as a harbor master.

Decades later he can only lament how the city has gone downhill. We are pleased when they enter the VIP section of the ferry and we can enjoy the journey over to Zanzibar sitting outside with the locals. Zanzibar is part of the United Republic of Tanzania but remains a semi-autonomous region. For this reason it has its own flag, and passports must be stamped as you enter.

We are greeted by a 'CHUMBE BRIAN' sign and driven to a small passenger boat, a wading distance from the shore, waiting to take us out to the island. Chumbe is a pristine island and part of the first marine park in Tanzania, so the snorkeling is amongst some great coral and colorful fish. Everything on the island is designed to protect the fragile environment and it's a true eco-tourism resort – a natural destination which is culturally sensitive, promoting an environmental awareness through education, and training and creating jobs for local people. The seven palm-thatched bungalows all face the beach and are constructed entirely of local material and are completely self-sufficient with water, catching their own and filtering it naturally through plant beds. Competent former fishermen have been trained as park rangers and they look after us extremely well during our stay. Accommodation is all inclusive and the meals are sensational, all served from hot dishes cooked on jikos by John King, the chef.

Each table overlooks the ocean from the 'dining room', an open area which is part of the old lighthouse keeper's residence, where a huge thatched roof has been constructed over what is left standing of the crumbling walls. The lighthouse, built by the British in 1904, is still in operation. There is also an ancient Swahili mosque on the island. It really is idyllic, and it's hard to remember when we have felt so truly relaxed, especially lying back on the hammock/bed on one of the quiet beaches watching the tide roll in. The island has a huge population of hermit crabs which you have to be careful not to tread on as you walk around the island. There are also a number of endangered giant coconut crabs which are nocturnal and quite forbidding if you encounter one as you walk back to your bungalow after dinner.

★★★

Back on Zanzibar Island we share a taxi into Stone Town with two of the guests from Chumbe, a mother and daughter from England. The mother's late husband had worked for Shell in Nigeria and Gabon in the 1980s. They have been staying at the Tembo Hotel and we find there is a suite available overlooking the ocean towards the mainland, and we cannot resist. It has a wonderful view of the Zanzibar dock area, so plenty of activity to watch from our balcony. It's a dry hotel, but that merely necessitates a short walk for a sundowner to the Africa Hotel, formerly the British Club, which is a popular venue at sunset and has a great atmosphere. Denise, wife of the owner, parades around with a pet monkey on her shoulder.

We explore historical Stone Town, where the Arabs initially built garrisons and the first mosque before the Portuguese arrived at the beginning of the fifteenth century. The Sultanate of Oman regained control 200 years later, when plantations of spices were planted and Zanzibar Island also became the center of the Arab slave trade. There is plenty to look at in Stone Town, including a wander through the vibrant markets.

Both nights we eat at the Forodhani Gardens food markets where dozens of vendors erect food stalls every night of the week, and under lanterns grill meat, fish, chicken, lobster, calamari and prawns served with salad or chips. Jikos are everywhere. The locals flock here each evening from about 6 pm and the atmosphere is friendly with lots of families and people of all ages enjoying the cool night, sitting along the promenade eating. We mainly eat seafood, but also try the crushed sugar cane syrup and a chocolate and banana pizza for dessert, which is more like a pancake. Tourists are actually in the minority but amazingly we run into people we have met previously, like Arch, one half of the Dutch couple who are here for a wedding, and Omar from Egypt and his Australian girlfriend Bridget, whom we met just before leaving Mikadi Beach.

We organize the obligatory Spice Tour and learn about the different spices and the features of each plant. The tour finishes with a local lad climbing high in the tree to fetch a coconut and expertly cut it open for a taste of the juice and the coconut flesh. The must-have photo is taken of the Spice King and Queen looking ridiculous wearing all the amazing palm leaf accessories they have made for us during the tour – royal crowns for our heads, a tie for Brian and a shoulder bag for me. On the way home we stop at the ruins of the Marhubi Palace, which was built by the third Arab Sultan of Zanzibar.

Back at Mikadi Beach Resort, we meet Maria and Bob, who have just arrived at the campsite. Maria was born on the island of Madeira, Portugal, however grew up in South Africa and her partner Bob is from England. Later they are to become the final couple to join our group traveling through northern Kenya, Ethiopia and Sudan.

Mikadi Beach is the first place we can remember hearing the Islamic *adhan* or 'call to prayer' on our journey north. The mosque is a short distance away and the voice drifts into our consciousness early in the morning. The *adhan* rings out from the minaret five times a day, prayer times determined by the position of the sun in the sky, but basically just before dawn, at midday, in the middle of the afternoon, just after sunset and at nightfall about two hours after sunset. Traditionally the *muezzin*, the most notable person in the mosque, was required to climb the minaret but more often these days a loudspeaker carries the message. Some seem more melodic than others and right at the mosque they are always loud but over time we become quite used to it, and from now on 'the call to prayer' becomes a regular audio backdrop to our travels through the Muslim countries to the north.

★★★

Huge plantations of sisal grow in neat rows far across the hilly landscape on the way to Peponi Beach Resort south of Tanga on the Tanzanian coast. Traditionally used for rope and twine, sisal is now also used to make paper, cloth and wall coverings. Dickie, Claire and their girls and Bob and Maria are already camped there. Bob has bought a huge fresh fish from one of the local fishermen, and he cooks a great fish curry for us all to share. They all leave Peponi before us but we will see them all again closer to Christmas.

Peponi is quite a perfect spot. Located right on the beach, it offers shade, cool sea breezes, a restaurant with great seafood, and good facilities, and the neighboring guest house sells fresh bread daily, espresso coffee (with ice cream extra) and sells clothes designed on site made from *kikoi* and *kanga*. Another surprise in Africa!! *Kikoi* is the traditional cloth that the fishermen wrap around themselves and is exclusive to the East African coast. A *kikoi* is made from 100% woven cotton with a design of bright colored bands and the fringe is twirled and knotted. These days the fabric is used for anything at all and worn by anyone and is very popular with tourists. A *kanga*, from the Swahili word 'to wrap' is similar to the *chitenge* worn in Namibia, Zambia and Malawi. A piece of colorful printed cotton fabric with a border along all four sides, it features a message or *jina* written in Swahili along the lower border. I buy one in black and red featuring a Tanzanian proverb which means 'Give a present from the heart'.

It is extremely hot and humid, we are now only three degrees south of the equator, but we relax and from our campsite watch the comings and goings of the locals from the fishing village nearby as they walk past on the beach – more of that watching-the-tide-roll-in type of inactivity. In fact, one morning we wake up to see a fishing vessel washed up onto the beach by the wind and high tide during the night and it is tilted and totally stranded. It becomes a hive of activity all day as the high tide is anticipated, at which time about a dozen young and able local men use all their strength to push it back down the beach into the ocean. One night at Peponi we celebrate Brian's 60th birthday with a meal of mangrove crabs at the restaurant.

★★★

The Marangu Hotel is at the foot of Mt Kilimanjaro and provides a small camping area out the back. Many climbers stay here before they set off on their big six-day climb and we chat to a few who are set to start their climb tomorrow. They are filled with anticipation and excitement. We only manage a glimpse of the great mountain from our campsite, as it is constantly shrouded in cloud.

The overlander travel tip for Arusha, the gateway to the Serengeti, is to stay at Maasai Camp on the edge of the city, a campsite with the usual backpacker accommodation, bar and restaurant. On weekends it is popular with locals with a disco on Friday and Saturday nights and the music is deafening until the early hours of the morning.

Arusha is busy, bustling and choked with traffic most of the time, hardly equipped to cope with the increase in tourism over the last few years, as well as visitors associated with the International Criminal Tribunal for Rwanda, established by the UN Security Council to oversee the prosecution of suspects in the 1994 genocide. According to the general travel lingo, Arusha's clock tower is the halfway point between Cape Town and Cairo, so it feels good to be halfway through Africa. Tourists can be targets so we are even more vigilant when leaving the vehicle unattended, pleased to have our security system and alarm.

★★★

In stark contrast to Ruaha National Park, the Ngorongoro Crater and the Serengeti National Park further north in Tanzania attract thousands of tourists. Despite this we have an unforgettable experience there, due mainly to the fact that it is the only park we view as passengers rather than driving ourselves in our own vehicle with no knowledge of African wildlife behavior and guessing blindly and often incorrectly which road might lead us to any animal sighting. Our local driver on the other hand is experienced and knowledgeable, regularly touching base via his two-way radio with other tour guides who are driving vehicles or overland buses full of tourists with hit lists of must-see animals.

No matter your choice of transport or accommodation in the Serengeti, it is all over-the-top expensive. To drive a foreign vehicle into the park costs a huge amount, with entry and camping fees very high, and by all reports the camping is very basic. We have also heard from numerous overland travelers of the damage inflicted on vehicles by the appalling roads through the Serengeti, which are very rough and deeply corrugated from the constant tourist traffic. So we organize our 'safari' from Arusha, where we book through 'Safari Makers' and treat ourselves to accommodation in the Sopa Lodges rather than their camping option which is expensive anyway, and a break from camping seems timely.

We set off with our guide Abdul, a delightful, quiet and unassuming man, in a rough and tumble Toyota Troopie with two home-made sunroofs which can be removed to allow us both an elevated 360 degree view from a standing position within the safety of the vehicle. We are lucky enough to be the only passengers on this trip, which suits us perfectly and turns out to be a bonus. Abdul only has us to please and there is no time frame other than our own on our game drives around the park.

We are taken up to the rim of the Ngorongoro Crater, an ancient volcanic caldera 18 kilometers wide which attracts tourists for its population of so many species of wildlife, the animal density well preserved in an area which offers year round water and food. We stop for a breathtaking view of the landscape below, a huge hazy depression strewn with patterns of ant-sized animals. We will return to explore the crater on our last day.

From the rim of the crater we slowly descend towards the Serengeti plain, through Maasai tribal country, scattered with circular kraals of huts made by the women from mud, sticks, grass and cow dung, and surrounded by fences of thorny acacia branches or wild sisal grown to protect the cattle at night. The men wear bright colored Maasai *shukas*. A *shuka* is used as a blanket for warmth, traditionally hand woven and made from cotton. Red is a major color often blended with black or blue or another main color. Bright dots speckle the landscape which is dusty and barren towards the end of the dry season and after many years of drought. The men tend their very poor cattle carrying their herding sticks, or positioning them across their backs and shoulders with hands draped over while they watch over their herd. The Maasai live off their cattle, mainly the milk but also meat and blood. The women, often with shaved heads, are wrapped in predominantly blue *shukas* with bright intricate jewelry dangling from their elongated earlobes and colored beads around their necks. These Maasai have not abandoned this traditional semi-nomadic lifestyle even though they can only graze their cattle in restricted areas of the Ngorongoro Conservation Area. Other Maasai make a living out of tourism, trading in souvenirs or offering accommodation or tours of their villages. We are astounded to see so many Maasai men with mobile phones attached to their ears as they chat in their traditional clothing in the middle of this vast plain where it can be easy to forget that it is the twenty-first century.

Our packed lunch is eaten overlooking the Olduvai Gorge while listening to a lecture by a local employee of the little museum behind us. He outlines the significance of the archaeological site before us, also known as The Cradle of

Mankind. Discoveries of fossil bones and old stone tools in this part of the Great Rift Valley have increased an understanding of early human evolution. Most of the excavations were completed in the mid-twentieth century by the British archaeologists Louis and Mary Leakey, and from 1976 to 1981 Mary Leakey and her staff also uncovered the Laetoli hominid footprints at the bottom of the gorge, left in volcanic ash some 3.6 million years ago. We sit in silence gazing across the steep-sided gorge which exposes layers of geological history, and contemplate the overwhelming concept of time presented in this landscape.

The wildlife is still exciting. Along with the elephants, zebra are definitely a favorite. Zebra stripes never fail to look spectacular and they have a photogenic neck-nuzzling stance, each zebra resting its head on the other's neck and brushing off flies with their tails while keeping watch in both directions. Any wildlife sighting is still a buzz for us but on our hit list here in the Serengeti are 'the cats' – lion, cheetah and leopard. Back at Ruaha National Park we had an up-close view of lions, but sightings of leopard and cheetah so far have been fleeting and from a great distance. There is also the possibility that we might just see the southerly migration of the wildebeest.

On the way to our lodge on the first afternoon we see a leopard in the grass some distance away and watch as he climbs the branch of a tree, sitting silhouetted against the darkening sky, his tail hanging down over a branch. Big dark clouds have formed and just on dusk we are dumped with torrential rain. Within minutes the road becomes sheets of water and Abdul has his work cut out to get us to the lodge, with visibility practically nil as the rain roars and pelts down on the vehicle. It rains all night.

After two days in the Serengeti National Park all the items on our hit list have been ticked off. Leopard, cheetah and lion are all sighted on one day not far from our open-roofed Troopie. On one occasion we are so close to a lion that my instinct is to duck down into the safety of the vehicle thinking that he is about to pounce, but he is merely moving away. We watch a lion 'changing of the guard' where Abdul explains it is probably two young brothers disputing ownership of a pride. There is no fight, just a stand-over. We have the luxury of time and watch the stalking of a gazelle by a leopard, striving to be close enough before the burst of speed. Something spooks the gazelle and in a flash all is lost for the leopard. As we drive around it is great fun standing up above the vehicle, looking like true safari tourists surveying the wide magnificent landscape. Brian has the camera on the tripod standing next to us ready for any photo opportunity, and Abdul is happy to stop any number of times for us to endlessly enjoy the animal interactions unfolding in front of us until we are ready to move on. The camaraderie between the drivers is entertaining – "Dullah, Dullah" is how they call up Abdul on the two-way – and they laugh and chat in Swahili sharing the locations of the best wildlife. Once we see up to thirty vehicles at one sighting, but more often than not the wide open spaces are far less crowded.

We are a solitary vehicle within the visible landscape the day we witness part of the migration of the wildebeest, the largest movement of wildlife on earth. At about this time of year, November to December, over a million wildebeest and nearly half a million zebra migrate south returning to the Serengeti from the adjoining Maasai Mara National Reserve in Kenya. The migration north occurred back in June when the grasses of the

Serengeti were exhausted, but as soon as the 'short rains' begin, when it rains briefly but not every day, the wildebeest begin their great migration back down to the south to calve in the Serengeti. The wildebeest are accompanied by hangers-on, such as antelope and predators, but predominantly by the plains zebra. The zebras are complementary grazers to the wildebeest, eating different parts of the same grass. They also play an important role in the migration, as their superior vision and hearing can provide an early warning system of potential danger for the wildebeest. When given the choice, predators prefer the wildebeest meat to that of the zebra, although twice we see lions lolling about and gorged next to a zebra kill.

Abdul drives along a quiet road across an open plain of scattered acacia trees right through the middle of this grazing mass of grey dots on a panoramic carpet of green grass. Standing up in the Troopie we are completely surrounded by wildebeest as they slowly move across the landscape. It is an awesome sight and the air is filled with the sound of their grazing and their distinctive honking. In southern Africa, wildebeest are known as gnus due to this "gnu gnu" sound they make.

Our last night is spent up in the clouds at our lodge on the rim of Ngorongoro Crater and in the morning Abdul takes us down the winding track through the lush forest down to the floor of the crater where flamingos occupy the lake, pink and shimmering in the distance. This huge crater supports a rich diversity of animals and birds, but after a rewarding morning drive it is time for us to leave. Serengeti National Park and the Ngorongoro Crater did not disappoint and have lived up to their reputation for us, and we farewell Abdul with a degree of sadness – he has provided us with an unforgettable experience of a lifetime.

★★★

Arriving back in Arusha from the Serengeti on a weekend, we try another campsite to avoid the loud Saturday night disco music. Ilboru Safari Lodge is difficult to find, tucked behind a village above Arusha at the base of Mt Meru. After bumping along through the throng of people in the ramshackle streets of the village, thinking it couldn't possibly be close by, we finally stumble upon the front gate, and we are permitted to camp in a tiny corner of the gardens. Arusha caters for the tourist market as a staging point for safaris into the many national parks in the area, as does this lodge with its lush gardens, pool and restaurant. During the afternoon we see a local wedding in the gardens and that evening we try the local Swahili cuisine on offer: *Machalari* – stewed beef and green bananas cooked with carrots and green pepper in a peanut sauce; *Pilau Na Kiku* – Spicy rice with vegetables served with pieces of chicken.

Before we leave Arusha there is the usual grocery shopping to undertake and we have heard about 'Meat King', a butcher shop catering for westerners. We find the shop is also a gourmet feast of many cheese varieties, good butter and fresh eggs, and delicacies not usually found in our recent supermarket purchases. Meat can be a tricky item to buy in Africa, often hanging outdoors unrefrigerated and butchered on request, so all our meat is bought in supermarkets, but it is often tough and ordinary. 'Meat King' has Kenyan meat, regarded as superior quality to the local meat, though we try both. The meat is vacuum sealed so we buy as much as we can fit in our tiny freezer.

Desert Elephants a triple jump away - Namibia

Excruciatingly tight squeeze - Botany Bay, Sydney, Australia

Giraffe on the run - Etosha NP, Namibia

Epupa Falls - Namibia

Elephants day and night - Croc Valley Campsite, Zambia

Honking, grazing wildebeest - Serengeti NP, Tanzania

Gorilla in the mist - Volcanoes NP, Rwanda

Lalibel highland vista - Ethiopia

Lonely Jebel Barkal pyramids - Sudan

How far back to Khartoum? - Sudan

Additional photos can be viewed at www.jonesroadtrips.com

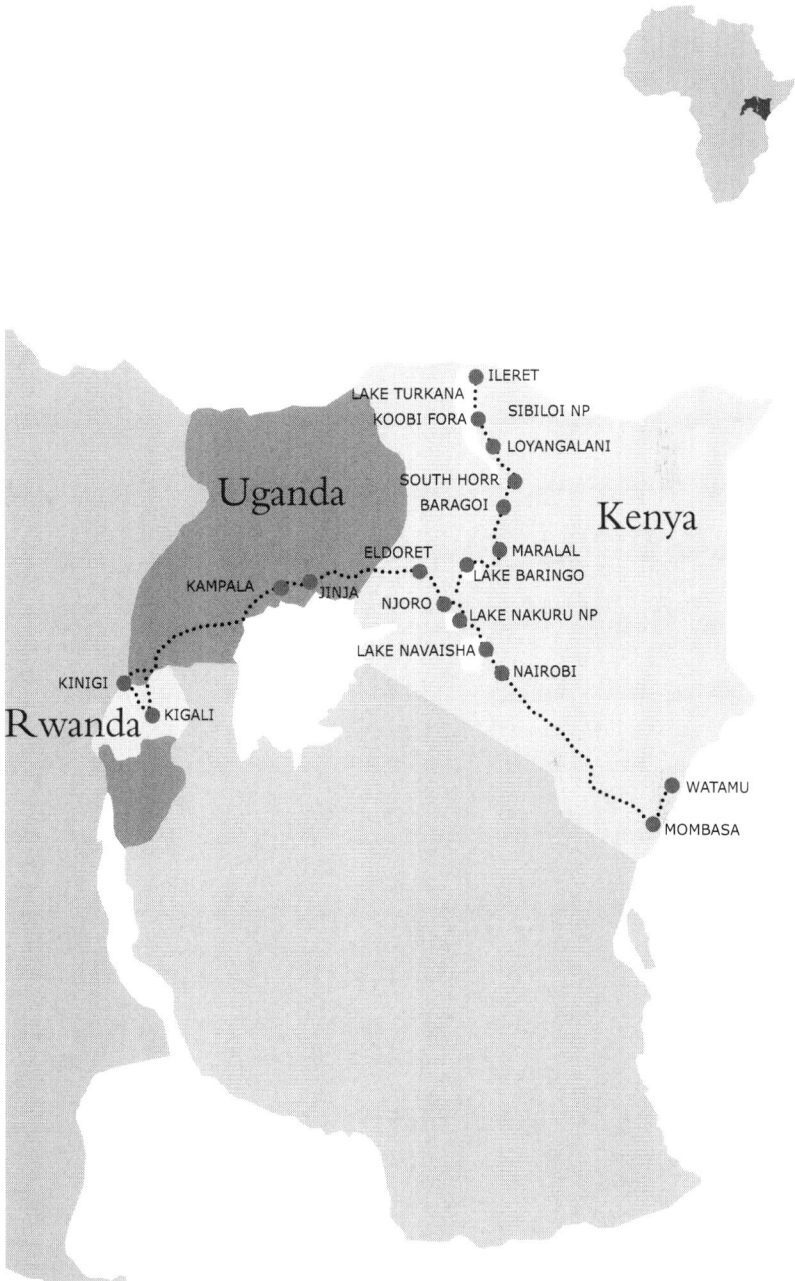

13.

Rwanda – banks, francs and gorillas, and the Genocide Memorial

The Rwandan border is a precursor to a country unlike any other so far. In complete contrast to the usual border turmoil, the efficiency of the Rwandan officials comes as a complete surprise, so smooth and well-organized it is almost spooky. After passing through the border boom gate, operated by a smartly dressed official who knows exactly the documents he wants to check, suddenly we are driving on the other side of the road after months of feeling at home behind the wheel. The road to Kigali, the capital, is perfect, following a valley through hills and mountains where every square-inch of soil is cultivated and terraced, even on the steepest slopes. Tea plantations add to a rich, green and lush landscape. All the roads we travel are in very good condition, and everything is clean and totally rubbish-free, tidy and orderly, so different to the intriguing chaos of the rest of Sub-Saharan Africa, where rubbish is an unmanaged problem and plastic shopping bags are a curse. We are led to believe that littering is punishable by hefty fines and even jail here in Rwanda, hence there is a foreboding sense of supervision, surveillance and over-management. But perhaps for a country that has suffered the devastating aftermath of genocide, to move on and forgive and live together again requires such an approach – who knows?

Our strategy of withdrawing local money from ATMs has been working well, and our account does not charge bank fees for these transactions so it's a satisfactory way to handle the money situation. Usually! We now know that Rwandan ATMs do not accept foreign credit cards.

Arriving in Kigali, our first priority is to drive to the Office of Rwandan Tourist Parks Nationale (ORTPN) to book our gorilla trek. Tomorrow is possible we are told, but when it comes to paying there is a blackout and the computers are down, so payment via credit card is impossible and regrettably we don't have enough US dollars or Rwandan francs despite managing to get a small amount in francs back in Kampala, Uganda. So we walk down to a Trade Center to withdraw from a shopping center ATM, only to find that it refuses our request. It is a Sunday and there is little open but we try at a bank ATM. Once again we have no luck. We walk back to ORTPN and the power is back on but Jackie, the parks employee, tries our card and it doesn't work. A fellow tourist tells us that he had the same problem and had to go to a bank at the airport to get US dollars to pay for the gorilla trek and Jackie says she will stay open until we return. Upon arrival at the airport we find the bank is closed and we are told at the information center that we can get money at a bank branch at the Novotel Hotel. We drive there but they can't help us and recommend another bank. We give up – the gorillas will have to wait until Tuesday. We take solace in a cup of coffee and pastry in the very western hotel and at least have enough money to buy a local sim card so we can phone Jackie to cancel our booking for tomorrow.

In Rwanda there is no camping, so we stay the night in the Hotel des Milles Collines of Hotel Rwanda fame, the film which depicts the Rwandan Genocide in 1994. The hotel has been refurbished and is quite impressive, with a smart reception area, comfortable rooms and an enticing bar near the pool outside. We have a sundowner and waiters mingle offering complimentary nibbles and taking drink orders, and we watch the promenade of older male expats with beautiful, young local women on their arms. There is a party atmosphere heightened by the melodious voice of a young Ugandan woman soloist, backed by an entertaining support band. We enjoy every minute.

Paying our bill the following morning is a trick, but thankfully our credit card works. On checking in, the tariff for the room was quoted in US dollars, but on checking out our bill is itemized in Rwandan francs. We pay by credit card and we are charged in euros. Brian laughs that we will not be the ones to benefit from any of those currency conversions!

The gorilla trek is booked and paid for the next day with our credit card which works this time. Our bank experience to secure Rwandan francs is far from straightforward. We line up in a queue to see the teller who directs us to a fellow at a desk out the back. Shuffled from desk to desk, we fill in countless forms until a bank check is issued which is signed and counter-signed by a progression of employees presumably moving up the hierarchical ladder until we queue once more at the bank teller who still needs more signatures behind the counter. Most of the morning has evaporated but we finally have some Rwandan francs!

The gorilla trek is to start at 7.00 am and the guest house at Kinigi is right on the edge of the Volcanoes National Park. Over dinner we chat to a young Australian girl from Byron Bay and her traveling companion from the USA, who have been doing some voluntary work in Tanzania, and have traveled through hell and high water across Tanzania, Lake Victoria and into Rwanda, all by public transport, in order to see the gorillas. At one stage they were traveling in a small sedan taxi, with five people sitting in the front and six in the back!

★★★

The first thing we see is his silver back suddenly visible through a break in the dense bamboo. He is in a crouch position, his stomach flat to the ground and his head steady as though he is having a nap. His back really is silver! A wave of excitement wells at the sight of him only five or so meters away, and then in the gloom we see the rest of the family going about their day as mountain gorillas do.

Mountain gorillas have thicker and longer fur than other gorillas, which enables them to live in the misty highlands of this part of Africa. The females in the group are eating fresh bamboo shoots or sitting around with the young gorillas amongst them. The only sound is the rustling of vegetation being torn away or crunched underfoot, and occasional bird sounds. But the most extraordinary thing happens right before our eyes. The silverback looks up and beckons to one of the females with his finger, and makes gorilla noises which must mean "Come over here", and we are suddenly witnessing gorillas mating in the mist. When all is done the silverback only wants to sleep, of course, his head tucked away so we hardly see his face again. He only glances up if he is disturbed by the young ones or by an interested female who is promptly ignored. The young juveniles start to play, chasing each other up bamboo canes that topple with their weight until they fall or jump back to the ground only to scoot up another one. They love this game and surely that noise they are making is laughter. The mothers eat on regardless, their huge brown eyes intent on their meal, and gorilla life unfolds as though we are invisible. We are enthralled and cannot believe it when the guide starts motioning to us all to start moving away – our sixty minutes is up! But what is really funny, after we have left the gorilla family behind and we are climbing back over the dry stone wall which forms the park boundary, one of our group has managed to film the whole event and announces she now has 'gorilla porn' in her possession!

The gorilla trek is a highly organized affair and worth the exorbitant permit fee. Before tourists arrive trackers seek out and locate groups or families of gorillas and radio in their location to the guide. They try to ensure everyone sees gorillas but nothing is guaranteed. Each guide looks after eight people on a quest to find one gorilla group and a ranger follows with an AK47 – just in case he's needed. Our group is called Group 13, an unimaginative name compared to the others, but our guide assures us it is a very special group. The silverback, the dominant male, is called *Agashya* meaning special, because he took over the group as a blackback – not yet matured into a silverback – and the group which numbered thirteen at that time, has now increased to twenty three quite quickly, a fact not lost on us during our allotted one hour with the gorillas. We walk through villages and cultivated rows of potatoes and pyrethrum daisy before reaching the park boundary, and the local children carting water in plastic yellow jerry cans call out, "How are you? How are you?" They are used to visitors.

★★★

The Rwanda Genocide lasted 100 days and left approximately 800,000 dead. The Hutu and Tutsi are two peoples of Rwanda who share a common past. The people who first settled Rwanda raised cattle and soon the people who owned the most cattle were called 'Tutsi' and everyone else was called 'Hutu'. Initially, interchanges between the two groups were common through marriage or cattle acquisition. With European colonization, the terms Tutsi and Hutu took on a racial aspect. Tutsis were favored for roles of responsibility because they had more European characteristics, such as lighter skin and a taller build, though they constituted only about 10 percent of the population. Animosity between the two groups continued for decades, and culminated in April 1994 when the president of Rwanda was killed after his plane was hit by a surface-to-air missile and crashed in Kigali. Hutu extremists began the killing spree using mostly machetes, clubs or knives. Men, women and children perished – perhaps as many as three quarters of the Tutsi population were murdered as well as thousands of Hutu because they opposed the killing campaign and the forces directing it.

We know the Genocide Memorial Museum will be harrowing, but because it's a part of this country's recent history and in our recent memory, we hope it will provide a greater understanding of the people and why it happened – it does. On arrival, to avoid a large group ahead of us, we go first to the exhibition on the floor above, where the stories of many of the genocides of the last century or so across the world are told: the Herero people in Namibia very early in the 1900s; Armenia in the early twentieth century; the Holocaust in Germany during World War II; the Pol Pot regime in Cambodia in the 1970s; and Bosnia in the 1990s. This part of the museum places the Rwandan genocide within the much bigger perspective of human behavior and tackles the questions that inevitably arise following these events. It is a sobering introduction to the exhibition waiting below. The whole experience is traumatic and exhausting. The museum depicts this incredibly tragic and horrific event with graphic images of the slaughter and nothing is spared. As we leave, a group of local Africans are also leaving, tears streaming down their faces.

At the Chez Lando Hotel, we relax on our balcony before setting off for dinner and watch a scene unfold before us. It appears two families have each just adopted a young child, presumably Rwandan. They are western families all smartly dressed and both the African children are wearing brand new clothes and shoes and their new brothers and sisters are so excited, running and playing with them. Each family poses for a photograph and then the children take turns nursing the new addition to the family. The two adopted children look completely overwhelmed with all the attention.

14.

Uganda – bananas on bicycles, Ankole cattle, equator crossing and the source of the Nile

By the time we cross into Uganda, we are becoming seasoned border crossers and we have learnt that patience pays off. Remaining polite and calm in all situations diminishes an official's tendency to exert his power. It's almost as if they are worn down by patience and courtesy and that they would prefer uncontrollable ranting to fuel their confidence and superiority. When they try to charge us for importing the vehicle, we are calm and confident enough to challenge this with our carnet. When they demand we pay road taxes (always a minimal amount) we are not deterred, and when they demand the taxes are paid in local currency, not US dollars, we calmly ask where we can acquire some local currency. There is so much mucking around and traipsing from one office to another but we are patient (outwardly at least). We have learnt not to rejoice a successful border crossing until we have traveled for at least another half an hour. Roadblocks are common and passports and documents can be asked for on many occasions along the road after a border.

Bananas, bananas, bananas – it is banana harvesting time. Rich, tropical hillsides are covered with them. Bananas crowd the roadside stalls and tomatoes and onions are delegated to the back crates. Mountainous loads of bananas overflow from trucks and most vehicles have at least a bunch strapped somewhere. But again it is bicycles that are tested to their limits laden with huge bunches, up to four at a time, strenuously pushed up hills, and then careering recklessly down the other side. We are now convinced there is not a thing that cannot be transported on a bicycle. In amongst the mayhem of bananas we see a timber double bed frame AND mattress strapped onto the back of a bicycle, balancing precariously but moving along triumphantly and taking up as much room on the road as a car.

At the equator it is a touristy affair with cafés and vendors' stalls selling souvenirs and food. A monument right on the hemisphere dividing line provides a touristy photo opportunity that we can't resist, one foot in the north of the globe, the other in the south. We are starting to notice the cattle with the largest horns we have ever seen. They are called Ankole cattle, and have a long tradition of being highly prestigious possessions. They have varied and interesting skin patterns and colors, each one known by a different name.

Jinja is situated on the shores of Lake Victoria, which is arguably the source of the Nile. The very spot that claims this fame, where the Nile River empties out of Lake Victoria, is not marked on the GPS so we have a few laps of the back streets of Jinja searching for it. The plaque at the site declares: "THIS AREA MARKS THE PLACE FROM WHERE THE NILE STARTS

ITS LONG JOURNEY TO THE MEDITERRANEAN SEA THROUGH CENTRAL AND NORTHERN UGANDA SUDAN AND EGYPT." This is the White Nile. The Blue Nile, which is the other tributary, starts in Ethiopia and they join up in Khartoum, Sudan.

Nile Explorers Campsite at Bujagali Falls has a bar/restaurant with outdoor seating and a view down over the Nile. While we sip coffee or enjoy a beer or a bar meal, we take in the spectacle of the rapids and kayakers practising their maneuvers below. But we won't brave the rafting – the idea of being dumped by the rapids is terrifying and if we need another excuse it's that we want to keep fit and well for the long road ahead.

We speed bump our way to Kampala, so many speed bumps, huge potholes and mad crazy drivers. Once again we stay at a campsite right in the middle of a big city. Red Chilli Hideaway is advertised as "The hottest place to stay in Uganda" and popular with backpackers and overland trucks. We brave the chaotic Kampala traffic to visit a couple of shopping centers to tackle a list of jobs as well as stock up on groceries. On returning to our vehicle, which is wearing much of the grime from dusty African roads, we find a finger-drawn message beaming at us from above our number plate and AUS sticker, next to our little kangaroo: "G'DAY FELLOW AUSSIE. HAPPY TRAVELS!"

15.

Kenya – visa quest, bribery, a coastal Christmas, floods and AK47s

Driving overland provides a valuable opportunity to observe the similarities or changes either subtle or stark between countries – a joining of the dots so to speak. Entering Kenya, the differences are immediately obvious – Kenya feels more westernized with many building construction sites and road works. Kenya is one of the most industrialized countries in East Africa, even though agriculture employs over eighty percent of the population.

A meeting hub for every overlander on the African continent – that's how it feels at Jungle Junction or JJs. The owner Chris from Germany arrived here years ago as an employee of BMW, but now his life revolves around a constant stream of overlanders gathering at his welcoming haven in the middle of suburbia in Kenya's capital, Nairobi. A two-storey house serves as a backpackers' hostel in the middle of a large security-fenced yard where vehicles, motorbikes, trucks, tents and campers of all descriptions and from countries all over the world find themselves a patch of ground and make new friends, exchange travel tips, explore Nairobi, apply for visas and have a much needed rest. There is even a mechanics workshop constantly busy with any number of tinkerers milling around bikes and vehicles.

When we hear that many fellow overlanders are managing to secure their Sudanese visas at the embassy here in Nairobi, we decide to try and take advantage of the opportunity, just in case something goes awry in Addis Ababa. Rather than drive our vehicle, we take a taxi. Our first port of call is the Australian High Commission where we request a Letter of Introduction to enter Sudan. It turns out that the letter just states exactly what is recorded in our passports, nothing more, nothing less, but apparently this is the hoop we need to jump through, so we do. The Sudanese Embassy is our next stop and, with our important letter safely in our hands, we arrive at 10.50 am to see that 11.00 am is closing time for visa applications. As we rush around filling in forms, a very surly looking Sudanese woman looks on from behind the window. We manage to submit our application and are told to pick up the visas at 2.00 pm on Monday. Today is Friday so all seems okay.

On Monday, another taxi takes us to the embassy, and we successfully pick up our visas. It is not until later we realize the date of entry is incorrectly written for a whole month earlier than we can possibly enter Sudan. We wonder if we can just change it, but that seems risky, so yet again the next day we head to the Sudanese Embassy. This time we drive ourselves and park at a shopping center nearby, catch another taxi from there, and present ourselves at the window to the same Sudanese woman, whom by now we know a little better. We explain our situation, and lo and behold, she uses 'white out' and changes the date! Appalled, we ask her if she is sure that we will be able to enter with an alteration such as that on the visa in our passport. She says, "No problem!" so we leave, thinking we could have done that ourselves!

There is no taxi in sight outside to take us back to the shopping center, but a very well dressed African lady whom we saw in the embassy offers us a lift back. Later we contact George in Khartoum to advise him we have secured our visas, and that we are still looking forward to our stay with him at the Acropole. We know that we will probably still be paying for any work that George has completed so far but it still feels good to have the visas.

The Ethiopian visas are next on our list to try to obtain in Nairobi. We now know that many embassies only allow visa applications in the mornings, so ideally it is best to arrive early and be waiting for the gate to be opened. Unfortunately we arrive at the Ethiopian Embassy late. We arrive prepared with photocopies of all our documents, but this embassy has demands we had not imagined, such as a blank copy of a carnet page, and there is no photocopier at the embassy that we can use. We also need to deposit the money for the visas in their account with the Bank of Africa, which is too far to walk from the embassy. Midday closing time is looming. We frantically drive to a hotel car park near the bank, scramble to find a photocopier, pay the minimal fee at a counter, wait in queues, fill out forms to be signed by waiting pens at various desks, and dash back to the vehicle. We have five minutes left for a ten minute drive. *Surely they won't be closed. What's that saying I have heard? We have the clocks but Africans have the time. Please don't let that iron gate be closed!* But it's 12.10 pm – and yes, the gates are closed! We park the car and walk over, forlorn and downtrodden, and peer through the bars but the warden doesn't want to know us. For a few moments we stand there envisaging yet another day plagued with officialdom and bureaucracy. The next day, determined to be first in the gate, we wait patiently outside until the gate opens. Within minutes we have our Ethiopian visas in our hands.

The Egyptian visas are still on our minds. *Why not try here for them as well?* Our border crossing into Egypt will be in the middle of Lake Nassar, and Bruno will be following on a separate barge. This may not be a challenge at all, but it would feel immeasurably better to have the visas in our hands when we arrive. We set off to find the Egyptian Embassy from the address in the guide book. This is one of the times we discover that addresses printed in guidebooks are not reliable. We find the appropriate building and foolishly squash into a crowded elevator to the seventh floor only to be informed that there is no Egyptian Embassy in the building. It is only when we are walking back out in the street that Brian discovers his wallet is gone, removed from a front pocket of his trousers. He remembers being distracted by a young child, perhaps the decoy for the perpetrator, or even the perpetrator. Luckily the damage is minimal, with only a small amount of money and no credit cards in the wallet. But all in all, definitely a day to forget because subsequently we become even more lost while we continue the search for the embassy and find ourselves in a part of Nairobi we sense is better to avoid. It feels suddenly seedy and we quickly backtrack and find refuge in an Intercontinental Hotel, regrouping with a very expensive cup of coffee before making our way back to our vehicle and the safe haven of our campsite.

Correct address in hand we drive to a leafy suburban area of Nairobi the following day. We park outside, a little uncertain about the very narrow street, but manage to position our wheels on the kerb to avoid blocking any traffic. Through the iron bars of the huge gate we ask if we can enter to apply for visas. It is quite an impressive embassy with a pleasant office for visa applications, with coffee-table books filled with enticing photographs of iconic Egypt. We fill in all the necessary paperwork but while waiting in the obligatory queue one of the security guards rushes in warning everyone that he has seen vehicles being towed away in the street by some sort of parking official. Panic! Our vehicle is everything – our home, our transport, our haven. Forgoing our place in the queue we rush out into the street and sit in our precious vehicle while we work out our next move. The security guard comes to tell us if we move the vehicle closer to the embassy, it will be better. We are not convinced but we take his advice, and I sit in the driver's seat ready to take off if they come my way, while Brian races back into the embassy to continue our quest for the visas. I nervously watch two fellows across the road, busy with a small vehicle. A crane lifts the car onto its back wheels, it is chained up to the tow truck and in no time is towed away. Brian returns and we leave immediately, not wanting to test the situation any further. And he still has no visas! We must get them on the border!

Back at the camp the owner tells us it is a shocking fate to have a vehicle towed away in Nairobi. They take it to a compound, the location known only to the tow truck driver, who has to be located in one of a myriad of bars, and the longer this process takes, the higher the fee required to release the vehicle. At a later date, we are telling the story to a fellow traveler, only to find he had the exact same experience outside the Egyptian Embassy, except it was his vehicle being chained up as he raced out. He had no choice but to pay for its release on the spot.

★★★

Just out of Nairobi there is a spectacular vista of part of the Great Rift Valley below before we descend to the lakes. We are starting to understand why the Great Rift Valley is the only geological formation visible from the moon. On the way to Lake Naivasha we pass numerous fresh flower horticultural farms with rows of greenhouses. Floriculture is the main industry around the lake exporting fresh cut flowers daily to Europe. Unfortunately, the irrigation is reducing the level of the lake which is a concern and a dilemma for the government since the industry provides a large amount of employment for the local population.

Fisherman's Camp was recommended to us back in Nairobi and overlooks Lake Naivasha in a beautiful park setting of lush green grass with a canopy of shade from a stand of fever trees. An electric fence has been erected around the lake to prevent the hippos coming into the camping area at night – unlike Croc Valley in Zambia. Once again there is a great bar/restaurant so as is often the case lately we opt for a respite from camp cooking. Crayfish with chilies could not have been produced from our pantry and is very reasonably priced. It's a popular spot for picnics and we are entertained by a busload of school children and their teachers, and another of medical students having a graduation celebration and playing soccer after their picnic lunch. Often the resident black-and-white colobus monkeys with long white manes down their backs cheekily roam the campsite and jump on vehicles if there is no one around.

We drive right around Lake Naivasha, past 'Elsamere' of Joy Adamson 'Born Free' fame, and on to the main road between Nairobi and Nakuru with the normal hectic African traffic – cars passing on blind curves or hills, buses and trucks traveling way too fast, especially downhill, and homicidal *matatus* overtaking at speed in and out of vehicles and then stopping without warning to pick up passengers. *Matatus* are privately owned mini buses that are the major form of transport in Kenya. We reach Lake Nakuru National Park and purchase our expensive 24-hour permit. This park is famous for its population of flamingos and before the mid-90s there could be up to two million of them crowding the lake. Now, however, they are less predictable after four years of drought, but those that have flown in this year are still a beautiful sight. Before we leave we treat ourselves to a lunch at the Sarova Lion Hill Game Lodge which is perched on the side of a hill with a view over the lake and national park. We are starting to call these flings into upmarket lodges our 'out-of-Africa' experiences. They are worlds apart from the life led by everyday people in towns, cities and rural communities, however, such is the history of Kenya and British colonization. We are in the White Highlands, so named for the settlement of 60,000 Europeans taking advantage of the good soil and cool climate from 1939 until the mid 1950s.

Kembu Campsite at Njoro is another good stopover with fresh bread and eggs for sale because it's a working farm with mainly dairy cattle, and as the owner Andrew says, "We alternate between wheat and dust". They have missed out on the long rains for a few years so it has been very dry. Andrew is an interesting fellow, who for three months of the year works in the film industry throughout East Africa, and using his local knowledge and understanding provides advice to the documentary makers on logistics and locations.

A deeply pot-holed tarred road showing years of neglect slows us down before we reach the main road which crosses the equator into the northern hemisphere for the first time, though due to the high elevation the temperature is quite cool and brisk. This road to Eldoret is a nightmare crowded with big trucks and although tarred it has deep tire ruts and bumps – it feels like a never-ending fun fair ride. Eldoret is the hometown of some of Kenya's legendary runners, and due to the high altitude is an ideal training ground. It is also the location of violent scenes back in 2007 after the controversial presidential elections.

An overland truck driver at Kembu recommends the Naiberi River Campsite which is a few kilometers out of Eldoret, a fantastic place with great facilities for camping, as well as lodge accommodation, a swimming pool and beautiful grounds sloping down to a river. The bar/restaurant called The Cave has a great atmosphere, highly decorated with African curios and a central fireplace in the middle of a large eating area. We have a good meal and Raj Shah, the Indian owner, joins us afterwards and after chatting for a while invites us to visit his woolen mill and factory in town the next morning before we leave. We later discover Raj is part of one of the oldest families of Indian origin in the Rift Valley region.

Raj has some complimentary fresh vegetables delivered to our camp next morning and we buy a colorful red *shuka* from the little shop at reception before we leave to meet Raj in Eldoret for a tour of his factory. Ken-Knit manufactures a variety of woolen products including blankets of varying quality to suit any budget, and school sweaters with those distinctive colored stripes on the V-neck and band. These are supplied to schools in neighboring countries as well as Kenya where uniforms are compulsory. Justice, our guide, takes us right through the factory which employs 2800 local workers in a huge shed of noisy ancient looms. We also tour the woolen mill across the road, which takes us back to our merino sheep-raising days of the past. Raj is very hospitable and we meet his brothers and nephews, all involved in the family business. On Raj's suggestion we visit the local cheese factory and buy fresh milk and some different varieties of cheese.

★★★

People often ask us about bribery and corruption in Africa. Our view is that the human race is the same everywhere when it comes to power and money, and there is no more bribery and corruption in the countries of Africa than in any other countries across the world. The difference is that in Africa so much of it is blatantly out in the open, 'on the street' and in your face, rather than hidden or behind closed doors – it could even be described as less sophisticated than in many places in the western world.

In Africa roadblocks are widespread because police do not have the luxury of a police car. Unfortunately at roadblocks, once the vehicle is stopped we often become the victims of bribe attempts. We are always asked where we have been, and where we are going, and a bribe can be worded in a variety of different ways: "And what have you brought me from ...?" "You have a present for me from ...?" "You have brought food from ...?" "There are a lot of hungry people here in ... so hungry they are falling down. What are you going to do about it?" Quite by accident we discover a way to pass through these roadblocks unscathed. We always feign complete ignorance of the meaning of their questions, and in response to their every request, their confidence diminishing with each one, we just repeat where we have been, and where we are heading, sometimes adding that we are from Australia. Eventually we are waved on impatiently, possibly regarded as complete idiots, or perceived as too hard and easier prey can be found elsewhere.

This tactic continues to work in all the countries we visit where police are inclined to misuse their position of power, and become aggressive or supplement their salaries with bribes. Unfortunately it is fairly common. But we take the view that we will avoid paying bribes whenever possible, that it only perpetuates such behavior, and we definitely become more brazen and confident as we progress further into our travels. There is only one time when we succumb, and it is here in Kenya.

Our store cupboard now boasts some Kenyan tea from the wide expanse of tea plantations in Kericho, the home of Kenya's large tea industry and we are driving along quite happily at a speed of 80–90 kilometers per hour, which is about the fastest we tend to travel. Suddenly, we are waved down by a policeman who comes aggressively over to my passenger side and belligerently accuses us of speeding. We deny it knowing we were only traveling our normal speed, but he insists we are a pick-up truck and the limit is 80 kilometers per hour. No amount of discussion is easing the situation, and he is poking his finger into my arm and yelling at close range that we must pay 10,000 Kenyan shillings (over AU$100) and we will go to court if we do not pay. Our resolve is evaporating but we know we actually have very little in Kenyan shillings as we have just bought some groceries. Sensing we are losing this battle, we discreetly go to our US dollars only to find our smallest note is a big one, close to what he is demanding. It all happens so quickly, and when we ask him for a receipt he keeps up the tempo and shouts, "Then you must go to court!" We decide to cut our losses, and as we drive away he says, "*Karibu Kenya* (Welcome to Kenya)", and waves us off with a smile! As time passes we become more annoyed with ourselves for not managing the situation better. In time we accumulate more strategies to employ in such circumstances.

★★★

"Christmas on the Kenyan coast? Sounds good to us!"

Watamu, north of Mombasa on the Kenyan coast is where we have chosen to spend Christmas and we have booked a campsite at Oceansports Resort. Liz and Peter whom we met in Tanzania will join us on the coast in a couple of days' time.

The Nairobi–Mombasa road is mad with trucks and speeding cars rushing to the coast, and we pass many broken-down trucks, with the customary broken-off tree branches at intervals before and after the breakdown to warn oncoming cars, a great substitute for reflective triangles! There are quite a few Maasai villages along the way and we share the road with the usual mini-bus taxis and larger buses filled to the brim with passengers, stacked to double their height with luggage, belongings, charcoal and whatever else, and constantly braving the wrong side of the road.

Driving through the port of Mombasa, the road is choked with even more trucks, many being washed from buckets by their drivers while they wait to load or unload. But the drive north along the coast is peaceful and rural. The campsite at Oceansports is a complete shock, especially considering we had booked in mid-November. There are no other campers, in fact it feels like we might have been the first for the whole year. The area is neglected and although we were aware it would be situated behind the resort, we hadn't imagined it would be quite so far down the back – even past the staff quarters! It is hot, there is very little shade and here behind the resort there is no breeze. On the positive side, the bathrooms are clean and the showers are hot, and the resort itself is excellent – a great pool, great beach and views of the pretty coastline from the bar and restaurant with fish, prawns and lobster on offer, and the beers are not overpriced! So where do we spend most of our time? It is certainly not at the campsite. However, they are charging an unusually expensive camping fee, so we lodge a complaint with management, as do Liz and Peter when they arrive, and eventually we manage to negotiate a slightly cheaper rate.

Liz and Peter are good company, and we also meet a young family from Nairobi who arrive at the campsite on Christmas Eve. She is originally from France and his parents are from England though he was born in Zambia, and works for the UN. Their two young daughters speak both French and English and we watch them enjoy their Christmas morning under their little African made-of-wire Christmas tree, before we spend the day on the cool terrace of the resort watching a camel decked out in a bright red costume for camel rides and a Santa Claus with a black face peering out between flowing white beard and Santa hat.

We thoroughly enjoy the beach experience and swim often in the Indian Ocean, the beach quite protected by a coral reef offshore. We hire a boat to snorkel but visibility is poor and the coral is mostly dead, but there are some colorful fish. The beach boys take us amongst the rock pools at low tide to see the moray eels, which they lure out of their rocky crevices with fish tied to sticks. They are fearsome looking creatures with wide large mouths and sharp teeth, and the boys have names for them all – Barack, King George, Queen Mary.

★★★

Just as well we are leaving in the morning!

On the last evening of our Christmas break at Oceansports, we are invited to join a cocktail party at the bar. We are introduced to Sally from England. Just a short distance further down the beach, she and her husband, sons, daughters and partners had rented a house which included a houseboy, cook, security guard and everything that should ensure a great Christmas on the Kenyan coast. She tells us that a couple of nights before Christmas just after they had finished dinner, six or seven men with machetes and AK47s stormed into their house and held them at gunpoint, forcing them to crouch under the table while one of their group was forced to gather up all the jewelry, money and valuables from all over the house. They were terrified and it is an experience they are all trying to come to terms with. Sally is still obviously traumatized as she is telling us, thankful that they escaped with their lives but unable to understand how the intruders had scaled the security wall without detection by the security guard and why there had been no response to the security alarm. It sounds like an inside job. The resort has taken them under their wing and is providing free accommodation until they can make their way back home. We think back to the two nights we camped by ourselves down the back of the resort. *Mmmm.*

★★★

After Boxing Day we brave the road back to Nairobi. This time there are far fewer trucks, but more buses packed with people returning after spending time with family over Christmas. We drive through the gate into JJs and are welcomed by so many people we have only met once or twice or not at all, that it feels like we have come 'home'.

There are four vehicles of overlanders making plans to drive through the Lake Turkana region of northern Kenya and cross the border into the Omo Valley of Ethiopia. Dickie and Claire and the girls in Dylan and Daisy, their Land Rover Defender and camper trailer; Liz and Peter in Boris, a Toyota LandCruiser wagon and roof tent; Bob and Maria in 10Bob, a Land Rover Discovery and roof tent; and finally ourselves in Bruno and the camper. Our departure date is set for New Year's Day. We are all back at JJs after Christmas to finalize preparations, stock up on supplies and set off on the more remote route east of Lake Turkana and into Ethiopia through the Omo Valley.

Our carnets for the vehicles also have to be signed and stamped out of Kenya here in Nairobi. We have been advised that due to the remote nature of the border, all paperwork for the vehicles must be processed before arrival. We all pile into a *matatu* and set off for the Motor Registry in Nairobi. It is a lengthy process of waiting and showing patience, just the normal, until our carnets are signed and stamped out of Kenya. At least the vehicles are ready for Ethiopia.

★★★

Our biggest supermarket surprise is in Nairobi in the suburb of Westgate where we first discover the Nakumatt 'super' supermarket, spread over two floors of the Westgate Mall. Nakumatt is a privately held company owned by Indians and the company has constructed malls throughout the Nairobi district, all with Nakumatt supermarkets. Anything you desire can be found in a Nakumatt supermarket. The unusual name is derived from the humble early days of the business when it was called Nakuru Mattresses. It is now a multi-million dollar business.

Hours are spent at the Westgate Mall in the next few days. We know there will be little access to money machines as we travel in the north of Kenya to the remote Omo Valley in Ethiopia, so we restock our supply of US dollars in an ATM blitz. We return over a period of four days, withdrawing our daily limit of Kenyan shillings at the ATM and then exchanging Kenyan shillings for US dollars at a foreign currency exchange. Meanwhile, we become familiar with all that is on offer at this very upmarket Western-style mall that caters for foreigners and the wealthy of Nairobi. Within the walls of this glitzy complex are theaters, a wide choice of banks, hairdressers, designer label boutiques as well as Western clothing chains, and a tempting selection of coffee shops, cafés and restaurants, some of which are also familiar chains back home. Cappuccinos, flat whites, iced coffee, treats and delicacies or delicious lunches are all suddenly available. We buy groceries at the Nakumatt and bread from the fresh bread shops. Usually, we buy the fresh local bread from markets, but having so much on tap is a novelty for us in Africa. Nakumatt is definitely another 'out-of-Africa' experience. We do visit the Ya-Ya Shopping Center and others in Nairobi that are more downmarket, but Westgate Mall is a treat.

★★★

It is New Year's Eve, the vehicles are all fuelled, grocery shopping is completed and we all have enough food and water to last us at least until we reach Ethiopia, where we will probably be able to supplement supplies at the markets in small towns or villages on the way to Addis Ababa, the capital. We envisage it will take us at least six days to get to the Ethiopian border.

New Year's Eve in the kitchen area of JJs is celebrated in style but in moderation. Everyone contributes to a table spread, including Sabine and Burkhard from Germany who have just arrived at JJs and have been traveling for six years in their self-contained purple 4x4 truck. Midnight local time seems too long to wait with our early start in the morning, so we decide to celebrate our New Year with Omsk in Russia at 9 pm local time, because in actual fact Australia's New Year has already ticked over at 4 pm local time, and Germany and the UK – well, out of the question! Peter has downloaded Big Ben chiming at midnight so it all feels quite authentic to be in Nairobi welcoming in the New Year and singing Auld Lang Syne with midnight revelers in Omsk.

★★★

New Year's Day and early morning is filled with all the goodbyes and photo shoots before we leave. For the fifth and final time on the African continent we cross the equator back into the northern hemisphere and we camp at Roberts Camp on Lake Baringo, a beautiful Rift Valley freshwater lake. There are hippos and plenty of baby crocs on the water's edge which Brian discovers when he wanders down for a photograph of the lake, so it becomes a more distant photo of the lake. A huge downpour during the night means a late departure the next morning while we wait for tents and everything else to dry out. But once on our way, the scenery is spectacular – Cradle-of-Mankind-Rift-Valley landscape so rugged and remote it feels like we truly are in the heart of Africa. Following the rain, the roads are quite slip-slide and messy but with magnificent views back to the lake. We see no other overland travelers all day.

Maralal is to be our next stop for the night, but as we whittle down the kilometers, the roads become more treacherously wet and muddy. The Kenyan drought is over! At about 5.30 pm, just 18 kilometers from Maralal, we see a collection of vehicles and *matatus* ahead. There is a very swollen creek cutting the road, and more vehicles on the other side looking just as stranded as we feel. Dickie starts chatting to a policeman on our side of the creek, and all in all it looks like we might have at least a three hour wait until the water subsides enough to cross the now invisible bridge. The policeman also advises us against camping there for the night for security reasons, so we settle down for the wait inside our vehicles in the queue that has formed. A very short time later there is an absolute downpour which lasts about an hour while darkness sets in, and we are all huddled in our vehicles fogging up severely. Our three hour wait has suddenly at least doubled. It looks like we are in for a long night so we all make ourselves as comfortable as we can, preparing for the worst – the entire night in the front of the vehicle.

Amazingly, we are both asleep when Dickie knocks on our window at 2.00 am. The creek level has dropped substantially and a couple of 4x4s have already managed to cross. So quickly we establish our place in the queue. Hearts in our mouths, we all manage to safely cross the now visible bridge with a washout on one side of the approach. The vehicles that had been waiting on the other side have long ago given up the wait and gone back to Maralal.

Continuing on in the moonlit darkness, the road is still very tricky and we try to keep an eye out for each other which isn't easy with the chaos of vehicles madly overtaking each other. It is only guesswork as to whose headlights or tail lights we can see. But a short distance behind us we suddenly see the flashing headlights of distress and for the first time on the trip, we have to use our winch. 10Bob has collected a huge hole on the side of the road and has ended up with two wheels off the ground – a little un-nerving for Maria inside who crawled out quick smart. We pull them out with surprising ease, and are on our way again.

We limp into Camel Camp just outside Maralal at 3.35 am – an epic day!! Our initiation as a convoy is complete. Needless to say there are no plans to continue the journey in a mere few hours time, and after a substantial sleep in we wake up to find that it isn't a bad campsite, quite grassy if a little damp, and we spend the next night there as well. Camel Camp is the venue for a yearly October Camel Derby, which explains the camels in the yards each night.

Fuel is available in Maralal, so we don't let the opportunity pass, and on the way out we also call in at the police station to get information on the roads ahead and to check the security situation. We are about to drive through bandit country where there is tension between nomadic cattle herders in the arid border area. Charles the policeman from our episode at the creek turns out to be the Divisional Commander of the whole region and he is extremely helpful. He will inform the police at Baragoi, our next overnight camp, that we are coming through and he also advises us that although it is renowned bandit country ahead, at this particular time there is no threat or any need for an armed police guide, as the recent rains have eased the four year long northern Kenyan drought, as well as the tension in the frontier zones.

Taking turns each day to take the lead, we drive through mountains and up to an elevation of above 2500 meters, the road very slow going, rocky and jagged. Samburu people draped in Maasai-looking *shukas* in this much cooler climate, watch their cattle or goats, with masses of colored beads around their necks. The landscape flattens into dry, more arid, saltbush looking country with a green tinge and the road is smoother with no dust following the rain. We pass sun-baked, desolate looking villages, with what has now become a common sight – children with their hands outstretched asking for sweets or money even though we have seen only one vehicle all day. We stop for lunch in a little clearing and a couple of locals wander by but keep their distance. Towards the end of the day's drive we are high on a ridge overlooking a spectacular view of the Rift Valley floor below stretching away into the distance.

On arrival in Baragoi we have driven for six hours and covered 90 kilometers. The entire population of Baragoi, which isn't very many, seems to be watching our convoy pass through, and converges when we buy fuel at the local depot. One man kisses the bonnet as Brian is filling up, and walks right around the vehicle checking it out. The police had been advised we were coming and we camp in a very small area behind the Baragoi Police Station, occasionally approached by children or adults asking for money or sweets, or a request of, "Give me pen", by one little girl, until they are kept at bay by the security the police have provided for us for the night. The night is uneventful, not flash but very secure.

Once again the next day we are given the all clear on security and the police phone through to Loyangalani police to let them know we are coming, and shake all our hands warmly when we leave. The initial hilly slopes with red soil and plenty of vegetation open out to rugged outcrops and plains and the locals become more intrigued and intriguing. Herdsmen tending their goats are scattered across the landscape, and those standing near the road with the obligatory herding stick over their shoulders and across the back of their necks watch us drive past. Sometimes they wave, sometimes they do not. We stop for lunch in a dry creek bed, or waddy as Dickie calls it, similar to the dry creek beds in the Simpson Desert at home, a few trees providing the only shade.

South Horr is an eye opener full of contrasts. We drive past a tin shed with 'South Horr' scrawled on the roof in red paint, and presume this is the extent of the settlement. But further on there are more buildings and a few people standing around, and when we do a right turn … wow! A community of shops and buildings of timber and iron lies before us with people everywhere, sitting, standing and walking; men and women traditionally dressed adorned with colorful beads, mud-dyed hair and decorative headgear; and all looking, looking, looking at the four vehicles cruising by. We pass a school and laughing children in Western-style pink and blue school uniforms race to the fence and excitedly wave and scream and shout out at us as we drive past on the dusty road. And just out of town, adults and children herd goats, and when we don't stop to give them money or sweets some children angrily throw sticks or stones at the vehicles, and young boys aggressively wave sticks at us. Later Peter finds a herding stick lodged in his back spare tire. Not long afterwards an overland vehicle comes towards us, the only one we see all day, and we have a quick passing chat with the Italians traveling south.

Bob and Maria are leading the day we pass through a checkpoint run by the locals. We are behind Dickie and Claire with Peter and Liz at the tail end. We always keep a look out for each other, each vehicle usually slowing down to keep the next vehicle in sight. On this day Boris keeps dropping back, so we drop back and so do those in front. When we stop for a short break, we ask Liz and Peter if they are having trouble with their vehicle. But no, they are stopping to take photos and to look at rocks, so they suggest we don't wait and just keep going. We wonder if this is such a good idea, but it becomes the agreed plan.

Driving down into a valley we spot the checkpoint in the distance and as we approach we can see that there are men ahead, some in khaki gear and plenty of AK47s. We have started to see a few of these as we drive along, men with rifles slung over their shoulders, waving as we drive past. We even wonder if they are just an accessory with no ammunition – but refrain from testing the theory. 10Bob has pulled up at the checkpoint and our vehicle and Dickie's queue up behind, but there is no sign of Boris, the last vehicle in our convoy. Maria is a whiz with languages – she speaks about five including Zulu – and manages to convey to the men at the checkpoint that we are tourists and just passing through and we are waved on. Boris appears from behind over the hilly horizon just as we are driving away, and Liz tells us later that they get a huge fright when they see us all stopped at the checkpoint, and even have a plan to just drive straight through if they need to. *Glad that didn't eventuate!* Amazingly, when they do stop Liz asks for a photo of one of the men with his AK47, but he refuses.

The road passes through a panorama of boulders of black volcanic rock strewn across the plain on either side of the road and purple hills in the distance. We stop for a closer look and they are scattered evenly across the ground completely surrounding us. It is rugged – the whole day's drive has been rugged and remote, and incredible, and it feels like we really are out in the middle of nowhere, once again Cradle of Mankind scenery and you can almost imagine early man wandering across the landscape.

But there is more, and over a rise we are suddenly confronted with the spectacular first sighting of Lake Turkana, the world's largest desert lake, also known as the Jade Sea, aqua-blue in the hazy distance, with volcanic rocks right down to the water. The Omo River is one of three rivers which flow into the lake, and the only water loss from the lake is through evaporation. Occasional groups of small dome-shaped huts are dotted round the foreshore, where Nile crocodiles live in abundance. The smallest ethnic group in Kenya, the El Molo tribe, are the traditional fishermen of the lake, still dependent on the lake for their existence in this hot arid area, with constant strong winds as the lake warms and cools, and little rain all year round from sudden violent storms. The road follows the shore for quite some time, past occasional fishermen and up over a rise where unexpectedly we see a much larger settlement of domed huts. There are people milling around and a man of religion is kneeling and praying at an altar at one end of a long smoothed patch of ground, a blue cross at one end, a red cross at the other. It has been a day to remember – an unforgettable drive and another 90 kilometer day.

Our camp for the night is at El Molo Campsite at Loyangalani, part of a neglected hotel amongst palm trees and green grass in an unexpected oasis-like haven, with palm leaf enclosed facilities which are basic and only one shower is connected to water. There are a few scattered *bandas* and an empty swimming pool. Dickie, Bob, Peter and Brian walk to the police station to tell them we have arrived, and return to tell us the story of the politician they have just met, who is due back in Nairobi tomorrow for meetings. He has four or five bodyguards with him and they will drive through the night in his black Toyota LandCruiser wagon, on a slightly more direct route to Nairobi than we traveled, but still a mammoth drive to be there by the morning.

Loyangalani was the setting for the film The Constant Gardener starring Ralph Fiennes, and we hear that many of the locals were employed as extras. The film crew apparently contributed some of their earnings towards a secondary school in the town, and the film director made a further substantial contribution.

In the morning Boris doesn't want to leave, and Peter spends some time doing on-the-run repairs. The locals have laid out a display of local artifacts and I have time to buy a 'dancing necklace' of rows and rows of colored beads, and a string necklace of ostrich eggshells. We leave the lake shore and pass men and children now herding goats, and camels with ropes or bells around their necks for easier control. The day is huge, we cover 206 kilometers in

12 hours, however, this does include about an hour's wait at the Sibiloi National Park gate while they send for the ranger from the park headquarters to take our entrance fee, and we also have to tow Dickie out of soft mud on the road. The good-humored banter about LandCruiser versus Land Rover continues. We reach Koobi Fora campsite further round Lake Turkana within the national park, where we finally set up camp in the dark and stay for two nights.

The Sibiloi National Park was created to protect a large number of hominid fossil finds, initially by Richard Leakey, son of Mary and Louis Leakey of Olduvai Gorge fame in Tanzania. The Great Rift Valley is becoming more and more interesting as we travel north and the little isolated Koobi Fora Museum is worth the visit.

At the campsite it is hot but there is a thatch roof stone building used by the rangers and visiting anthropologists and archaeologists. There is a shady terrace where we can sit in the cool. After the museum visit Maria sets up Maria's Flapjack Café with the two girls, with name tags around a table and the girls are the waitresses and take our orders – flapjack with honey or flapjack with Nutella.

The day we leave it is our turn to lead. We are driving across the Koobi Fora Point and it's tricky. Since the rain only one vehicle has passed through here, the tire tracks only visible where the shale is still soft with moisture. Any semblance of a track is hard to make out, most of it washed away by the rain. The clay pan of shale bordering the lake area is an uneven surface scattered with patchy stands of low thorny scrub, and the wind is blowing dust which swirls around us and at times we cannot see Boris behind us. We often stop and hop out to check the way ahead. It is challenging driving and hard to tell where the surface is firm enough to hold our weight but we get through with hardly a problem and eventually move on to a gravel road further away from the lake for the rest of the drive through the Sibiloi National Park. On a rise overlooking Lake Turkana, just before the road descends down to the park boundary, we stop for lunch. Herders tend their goats and cattle as they graze on the fresh new grass interspersed with little wildflowers, some of which are the yellow flower of 'cat head', a weed that grows at home.

We reach Ileret mid-afternoon and report our arrival to the police. Our campsite for the night is at the back of a police station again, no showers and very basic, with the usual wide-eyed onlookers as we set up camp. But the police inspector is very friendly, and his band of 'policemen' gathers in a shed nearby to play a game of cards. We have another pleasant and secure night, though the donkeys are noisy.

In the morning we say goodbye to the policemen, shake hands, and set off on our last day in northern Kenya. Our most interesting and remote border lies ahead.

★★★

Little villages of domed huts reinforced with galvanized iron are spread all over the landscape and as we near the border we start to see bare-breasted women with layers and layers of beads around their necks, waists and arms and little children running around naked except for intricate beaded necklaces. The men carry their carved headrests while herding their cattle and goats.

It is only the GPS that confirms the location of the true border between Kenya and Ethiopia. A photo must capture this moment – we are in Ethiopia! We all park in a row exactly where we believe the border to be. It is a flat grassy area, and a couple of tribal men and women wandering by stop to watch the spectacle. This is the only border where we have ever taken photos – photos at borders make officials edgy – but here, not an official in sight. We have reached the Ethiopian border and it has taken us nine days, not six!

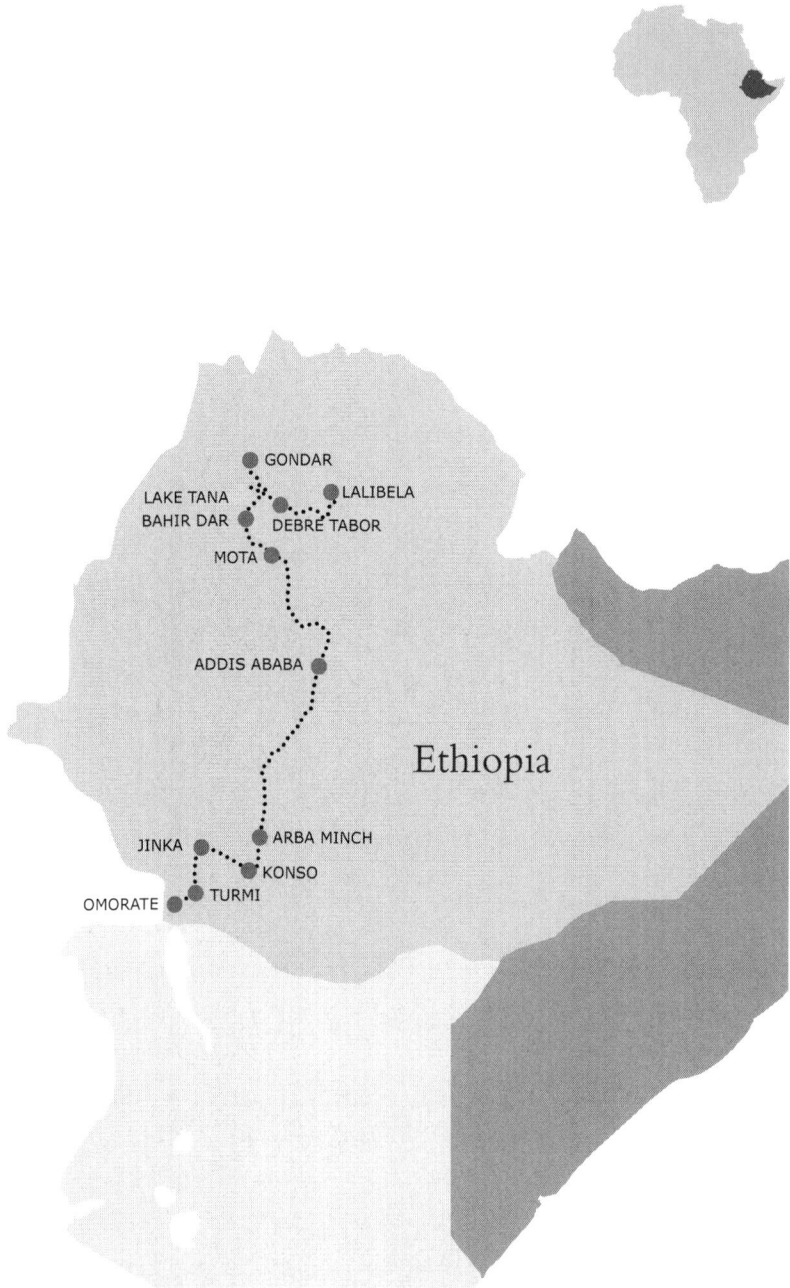

16.

Ethiopia – spicy cuisine, clocks and calendars, Omo Valley, Lucy's bones and rock-hewn churches

After our photo session, we climb back into our vehicles and it is not long before we reach a boom gate next to a tin shed. A crowd gathers quickly around us – we are all intrigued with each other. A young girl with scarring on her back peers into our side mirror, scrutinizing her appearance in the clear reflection we have provided. The local policeman has to be roused from a nap, and he dutifully looks at each of our passports as we squash into his 'office', while outside is a mini riot with all the locals and their children gathering, rather excited about our four vehicles. Our Police Inspector back at Ileret armed us with a letter stating that all is well with us leaving Kenya and we hand over the letter. Meanwhile outside, children are being chased away from our vehicles by a … policeman? There are no uniforms as such. All goes well, although the passports did not actually get their official stamp of departure out of Kenya. But we are on our way.

It is both exciting yet daunting driving through Ethiopia. From the border we drive through dry riverbeds and flat, hot country, with children running out of nowhere grabbing on to the vehicles wherever they can and running along while trying to hold on. Our greatest fear is that they will fall under the vehicle. Sometimes the older girls and boys stand in the middle of the road waving their arms to try and make us stop, so we have to edge carefully through them. Some children even throw stones and there are occasional displays of aggression – a woman shooing us away and a boy wielding a *woko* or herding stick at us as we drive past. In contrast, others wave excitedly and welcome us with huge smiles.

We are out of Kenya but our next challenge is to get our passports and carnets stamped into Ethiopia. There is a small village called Omorate on the Omo River, a slight detour, but this is the Ethiopian border town in this part of the world. We were told in Nairobi that we would have to go there, even though it is not on the road to Arba Minch and lies about 50 kilometers from where we took our border photos in the middle of nowhere. We eventually locate the small immigration/customs office, documents are stamped and we are officially traveling in Ethiopia.

Ethiopia has been our greatest surprise so far, certainly not the desert and famine that is often associated with this country. The vast majority of Ethiopians live on an elevated, very fertile central plateau called the Ethiopian or Abyssinian Highlands, and the landscape is truly spectacular, further enhanced by the Great Rift Valley. The Ethiopian clock has 24 hours in a day but the clock is configured so that the new day starts at 6 am rather than at 12 midnight. This makes sense given that Ethiopia is located near the equator and the sun comes up at the same time every day of the year. To convert between the Ethiopian and western clocks it is just a matter of subtracting six hours. Not that time is very important for this part of our journey. And Ethiopia works on a different calendar – the ancient Coptic calendar which is still in use today. Definitely a bonus – suddenly we are younger by nearly eight years!

We had heard about the stone-throwing children in Ethiopia from other overlanders and it is confronting and not pleasant at times. Children yell out, "You! You! You!" or "Give me pen!", "Give me money!", or "Sweets! Sweets!" They hold their hands out and point to their mouths and often chase the vehicles. It is a moral dilemma, as we do have so much and they have so little. On one occasion a young boy throws his *shuka*-like blanket at Dickie's vehicle and it becomes wedged on the bonnet but Dickie keeps driving. We are last in the convoy and by the time we pass the boy he is absolutely distraught, running and sobbing trying to keep up with the vehicles, in hysterical fear that he has lost his warm protection from the cold. It is a heart-rending sight, but thankfully, Dickie stops further up and places the blanket on the side of the road for the boy who is still desperately trying to keep up behind. It is traumatic for everyone.

Whenever we stop for lunch, within minutes we are surrounded, and on one occasion we see a traditionally dressed man in the crowd holding a machete. He is probably harmless but it gives us an uncomfortable feeling. Often we eat as we drive along, knowing the situation will erupt into chaos if we give out any food, though these people are not starving. The severe droughts occur down in the lowlands.

We see a young naked boy doing a handstand to try to attract our attention as we pass by. Young boys from the Karo tribe, their faces painted with pulverized white chalk, perform strange antics on the side of the road, a weird type of dance with arms and legs angled in an L-shape from their bodies as they crouch and jump up and down. And we even see two painted Karo boys walking along on stilts. It seems unlikely in such a remote place that these antics could be rewarded and encouraged, but there must be enough visitors or aid workers driving through for this to be the case. We know that tourists come down from Addis Ababa in four wheel drive tour groups, and are taken to villages to see the different tribes in the Omo Valley. We hear that the children ask for birr, the Ethiopian currency, and any photos taken require payment. These miniscule acts of giving make little difference to the lives of these people, other than diminish their dignity. Tourism continues to change our world. We are tourists but would prefer to just see life as it happens around us rather than search for the ultimate tourist experience or photograph.

And there is plenty to see along the road, as people go about their daily lives. Driving into Turmi, our first camp in Ethiopia, Hamer women wear headbands and collars of tiny beads in banded colors, and colored necklaces of beads or cowry shells, which hang low with the animal skins they drape over their shoulders or wear as skirts. Others wear their hair in hanging little droplets of mud and ochre, like a thick all-over fringe and women and children have metal and colored bracelets fixed tightly around their arms and legs, and beading around their waists. The women often have visible scarring on their backs and sides, another way to beautify themselves. Men love to colorfully decorate themselves as well. We see Hamer men wearing beaded headbands often decorated with feathers and Karo men with clay hair buns also with feathers and carrying beautifully carved wooden headrests and herding sticks. And it is on the road to Turmi we see our first road sign written in Arabic, and now *salam* is hello.

We visit the local market. People are walking along the roads into town pulling goats, or carrying huge loads of grass, hay, sticks or charcoal, and all manner of implements and produce. At the market, vendors have their wares arranged out on the ground, and everything around us heaves with activity. We buy another 'headrest' to go with our Himba 'pillow'. By chance, Burkhard and Sabine are also at the market. They have been traveling a day or so behind us. Not far out of Turmi on our way to Jinka a local car is axle-deep in sand in one of the dry riverbeds alongside the road. We stop to help and a crowd of onlookers and passers-by develops to watch us attach the winch and free the car, while we also have an opportunity to watch them and mill around the people at closer quarters.

Jinka is the first substantial town where we can stock up with more supplies and organize some local 'birr' at the bank. It is always more comfortable to have some local currency. Fresh local bread is always at the top of our list, especially by the time we reach northern Africa where the culture, people and food become more Middle Eastern than African. The bread is part of the culture and usually a major part of the diet. In Ethiopia, *injera* is part of the national dish, flat bread made with yeast and teff flour mixed with water and allowed to ferment for several days. It is then baked into large flat pancakes traditionally on a clay stone, and the base of the bread has a flat texture while the top is porous and spongy. It has a sour taste but its texture makes it perfect for scooping up stews and sauces.

Our campsite in Jinka is in the grounds of a small hotel. We negotiate with the owner for the use of the shower in one of the rooms for a reasonable rate, even though we all choose to camp and sleep in our own beds. The hotel has a little restaurant where we enjoy the first of many typical Ethiopian meals. Our favorites are: *injera* dotted with several kinds of spicy stews and sauces, so the 'plate' of *injera* is torn off in pieces to scoop up the meat until finally the plate is eaten and is by now soaked with all the different flavors; *Doro Wot* is a spicy chicken stew piping hot in a little black pot next to the *injera*; *Yebeg Tibbs* are lamb cubes fried traditionally in onion, garlic, ginger, green pepper, traditional butter, and Ethiopian herbs and spices; *Shiro Tegamino* is a thick paste of dried peas and traditional spices; *Bozena Shiro* is powdered dried peas with marinated beef. They are all very spicy and delicious.

Thatched huts with peaked roofs topped with various objects or designs – animal skulls, ceramic pots, crosses – are scattered through the hills on the road to Konso and at Arba Minch we find a hotel very late at night. It is too late to set up camp, having been held up on the road when a bolt broke on Dickie's coupling to the trailer.

The road to Addis Ababa becomes busy and hectic as we get closer to the city, with huge numbers of donkey or horse-driven carts often crowded with people, or donkeys overladen with produce, their little legs buckling under the weight. We pass mosques but now we see some Christian Orthodox churches as well with huge hemispheric roofs, often gold and white.

In Addis Ababa, the capital of Ethiopia, Wim's Holland House is there on Tracks 4 Africa on our GPS, but we just can't locate it. Wim's was recommended by other overlanders. We park on a busy six-lane road through the city and Brian wanders around and eventually asks a traffic policeman for directions. He tells us we must go the other way down this busy street before turning off and it is just around the corner. He says we can do a U-turn and Brian mistakenly thinks he is going to assist. But he turns his head the other way, so with a right hand vehicle driving on the right hand side of the road Brian somehow manages to do a U-turn across six lanes of traffic in the middle of a city.

Wim's Holland House is a friendly campsite run by a Dutch expatriate. Wim's is full of overlanders in a tiny space, but has a great restaurant where the traditional food is hot, spicy and excellent. On our first evening we are lucky enough to chat to some of the friendly locals who have called in to the restaurant for a few drinks after a wedding. During the night, the barking of dogs is constant, and before daylight the next morning, priests start their chanting and continue for at least a couple of hours. Ethiopia is predominantly Orthodox Christian and we have arrived in time for Epiphany, an important religious celebration on the Ethiopian calendar with a holiday to mark its significance, which may account for the length of the early morning call.

We opt for a hotel stay after a couple of nights, the spicy food taking its toll rather too severely, staying firstly at Jupiters and then at the upmarket Intercontinental. One day in the open-glass elevator, Brian embarks on some casual chit-chat with a man, asking him if he is from the area. He is surprised. He responds good-naturedly that surely he doesn't resemble the local people. It's a lesson to be learnt about light-hearted chit-chat. We have noticed a change in the features of the local population in southern Ethiopia, to a more Middle Eastern look and lighter brown complexion. We remember a taxi tour we once had of Alexandra Township in Johannesburg. The taxi driver was adept at identifying the different African races by their facial features, body size and dress. To our untrained eye they all looked very similar.

Addis is a typical bustling, overwhelming city, but fascinating! Men walk hand in hand or with their arms draped around each other, a culturally acceptable way of engaging in conversation as they walk down the street. Men and women greet each other by shaking hands along with a cheek to cheek three times, but without touching cheeks. Coffee houses are everywhere, supporting a very traditional coffee culture and most of the signage is in Arabic. There is the usual crazy traffic to negotiate and countless noisy building sites adding to the dust and chaos – with shoe shiners in the streets doing a roaring trade with the locals.

When we arrive in Addis Ababa one of our first tasks is to secure our Egyptian visas. Within two days we have them. We also lodge an application for visas at the Libyan Embassy, which we hope to collect in Egypt. Dickie enquired at the Libyan Consulate back in Dar Es Salaam and was assured that we can apply for a transit visa without a guide. Little do we know of the 'fun' we will have securing a Libyan visa in Egypt.

We have the car serviced and we must visit Bambi's. It is a supermarket run by Greeks that we have been told is worth a visit. We have great fun searching the shelves of unfamiliar products with indecipherable labels, but we still manage to stock up admirably. It's certainly not a Nakumatt, but it may be the best we see again for a while.

There are no ATMs in Ethiopia, but we hear there is one in

the extraordinarily lavish Sheraton Hotel. It was discovered by
Liz and Peter on a search for an internet connection. The serenity
of the foyer and the plush surroundings are in stark contrast to all
that pulsates outside. It is truly another 'out of Africa' experience
– but with great coffee and cakes!

★★★

A visit to the National Museum represents a farewell to the
Great Rift Valley for us. By now we are excited to view the
famous remains of Lucy, one of the oldest finds of human-like
remains for which the Rift Valley is famous. Lucy's bones are
displayed in a glass enclosure, and there is a standing model of her
whole skeleton extrapolated from the excavated bones, also in a
glass enclosure. We wander through the museum which is quite
rustic, and there is a display of a 60 second time line: one minute
representing the time that has passed since the most ancient
human lived over 400 million years ago (about 4,400,000 years
ago); accordingly 1 second = 73, 333 years. This means that on
the 16th second, Lucy was born, lived and died; on the 26th
second, the first real man appeared; and only around the 54th
second was fire mastered by man, who didn't look like modern
man until the 57th second. And the invention of writing, the
construction of the pyramids, and the events of the twentieth
century, all the events that make History, passed in a tiny fraction
of the 60th and last second. *Wow!*

Driving back from the museum, we miss a portioned-
off left-turning lane, but turn left anyway. Shortly afterwards
a policeman pulls us over and seems agitated, trying to make
himself understood by us while at the same time talking on his

mobile. It appears that he has received a phone call about our 'mistake' but had initially thought we had committed a greater offence. It is worrying at the time but it isn't long before he finishes talking on the phone and is happy to wave us on.

★★★

Ethiopia becomes deliciously cool as we climb to a height of over 3000 meters on the road out of Addis Ababa. The western clothing worn predominantly in Addis changes to the more traditional, the women in long cotton dresses and shawls, sometimes their heads covered with cloth, and the men in long shirts. The scenery is immediately spectacular, with rich fertile soil, and the countryside looks to be very productive, with people on their knees harvesting crops by hand with scythes. The sheafs are piled into bundles, which are then beaten on the ground to dislodge the grain, and they are then carried to be thrown onto one of many haystacks dotted across the landscape. Farming is not mechanized but everything seems so well managed. Even the cattle look to be in good order with their ever-present herdsmen draped in cream colored fabric with a green or pink shiny braid along the edge and carrying crooks across their backs. The towns and villages are neat and tidy without the usual rubbish and plastic bags in the street. We are also interested to see the huge numbers of eucalyptus trees growing everywhere – it feels like home. They are used for so many different purposes – firewood, the framework of houses before filling the gaps with mud, and the leafy branches make good fences. Donkeys and people carry huge loads of eucalypt branches which are cut at ground level, and then re-shoot in thin branches.

Mota and Debre Tabor are two hotels on the way to Lalibela, both painted pink, and we stay in basic but comfortable rooms rather than camp in the car park. Breakfast isn't included in the tariff, so two self-catered 'car park' breakfasts provide some entertainment for the locals. We drive down through the one kilometer deep Blue Nile River Gorge, and up the other side after crossing the impressive cable bridge built by the Japanese, and we have lunch at a resort in Bahir Dar overlooking Lake Tana, the source of the Blue Nile. Closer to Lalibela we are driving on a perfect new tarred road, expertly constructed by the Chinese.

Lalibela is 645 kilometers from Addis Ababa, high up in the Ethiopian highlands and is worth the two day drive. King Lalibela carved eleven rock-hewn churches out of the red volcanic rock in the late twelfth century. A local guide is compulsory and we spend most of the day on a tour. Four churches are completely free standing, attached to the rock only at the base. The churches are hewn with hammer and chisel, the chisel marks still visible and many are connected by small passages and tunnels. They are quite dark and somber inside, decorated with paintings or designs on the walls, though others are completely plain. It is a place of Ethiopian Christianity and to this day a place of pilgrimage and devotion.

We camp at Mountain View Hotel which is perched on the edge of a mountain overlooking the highlands as far as you can see in a 180 degree vista. Sunsets from the roof of the hotel are spectacular and a perfect spot to meet for a sundowner.

Gondar is our last city in Ethiopia, where we visit the Royal Enclosure which consists of a walled compound of seventeenth century castles and buildings built by Emperor Fasilada. We stay at the Goha Hotel, high on a hill overlooking the town, with a garden just perfect for our last sundowner before entering alcohol-free Sudan. We have been watching the staff all day prepare a beautifully decorated open tent draped with white satin and bright orange balloons and as sunset approaches we feel the excitement mounting. The bridal party arrives to a fanfare of loud music, the bridesmaids dressed in bright orange and the groomsmen with bright orange ties. All the guests pour in, and what follows is a lively celebration of singing, clapping and dancing. The guests don't have chairs, but sit around the cordoned-off pool wherever they can find a space, or stand around and clap and dance to the beat of the live music and singers. Ethiopian dance is all neck and shoulders, and the music is distinctively high-pitched. It is a great atmosphere and some of the guests come over to talk to us and want their photo taken with us. That night after dinner we share any alcohol left in our campers for little nightcap tasters before the Sudanese border in the morning.

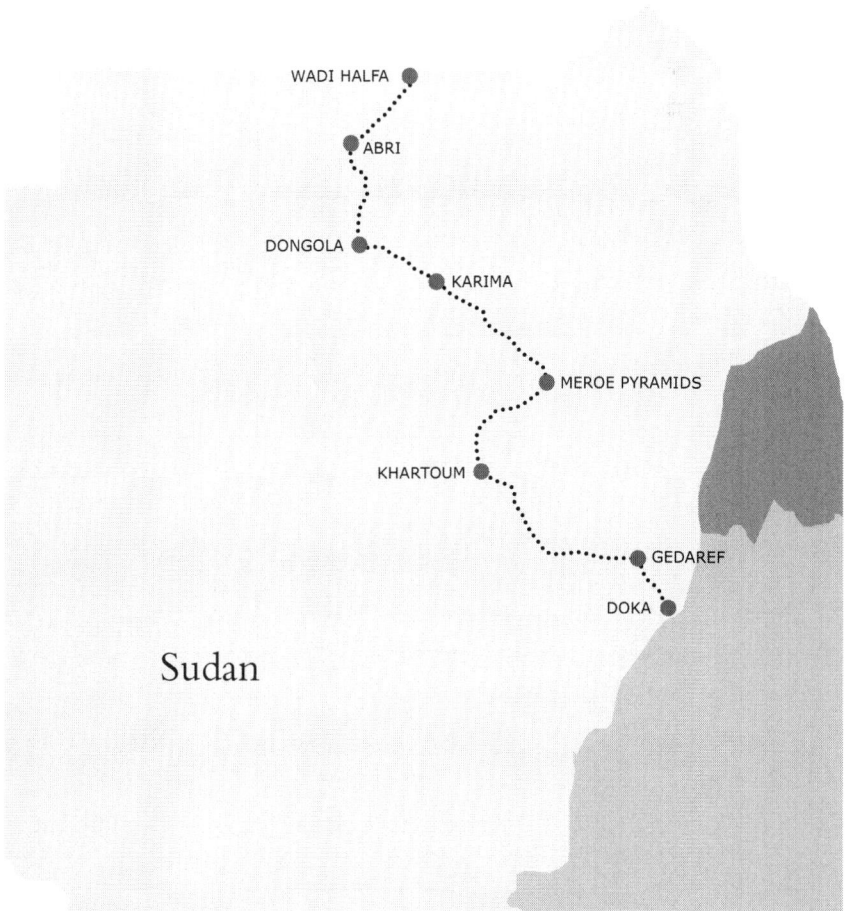

WADI HALFA

ABRI

DONGOLA

KARIMA

MEROE PYRAMIDS

KHARTOUM

GEDAREF

DOKA

Sudan

17.

Sudan – Meroe pyramids, Nubian Desert and barging into Egypt

Leaving Ethiopia we sit in a tiny immigration office while the official checks pages and pages to ensure that our names are not on his list, whatever it is. We are just glad our names are not there. On the Sudanese side we sit patiently in customs waiting for the official to at least look up from his paperwork. But we are on the road only an hour and a half later. Once again everything changes very quickly. We encounter so many roadblocks, mostly friendly and always asking for names and nationality, and very often requiring us to get out of our vehicle into a little 'office' by the side of the road, where we show our passports and they write down all our details.

The elevation changes dramatically, down from over 2000 meters to 500 quite quickly, and with it a huge rise in temperature after the coolness in mountainous Ethiopia. Now the landscape is of vast stretches of beautiful black soil open plains, obviously broad-acre farmed and harvested as far as you can see, until gradually the soil changes to a lighter colored chocolate soil as we approach the desert country.

The people also change as now we are again in a predominantly Muslim country in this northern part of Sudan after the mostly Christian Orthodox northern Ethiopia. The men are in white flowing robes and white head cloths, and the women are often in black from head to toe, but at the very least their heads are covered with scarves. The houses are now mud brick and square, in treeless compounds often with elevated 'cages' of earthenware pots out the front, obviously filled with the day's water supply.

We bush camp between Doka and Gedaref a short distance off the tarred road to Khartoum. It is very hot and with very little shade, and myriads of little bush flies disappear with our first spectacular sunset in Sudan, followed by a full moon. And it is all good fun camping with our fellow travelers, three vehicles still traveling together since Nairobi – Dickie and Claire and the girls; Bob and Maria; and us. Liz and Peter are spending more time in Ethiopia but we keep in touch with them for the rest of the journey.

Towards Khartoum the landscape becomes more arid and desert-like, the driving more glary and dusty, but an excellent tarred road. We head straight for Khartoum's oldest hotel, the Acropole, run by George and his family originally from Greece. Although we were able to secure our visas in Nairobi without George's help, he still proves to be of great assistance, organizing our travel permits and photographic permits for the drive north from Khartoum. There are no ATMs in Sudan either but George is our trusted mentor in all things Sudanese and changes our US dollars to Sudanese pounds at a good rate.

From the Acropole, we explore Khartoum during the day, catching the local broken-down taxis which George organizes for us from the hotel. One of our drivers, Tyeb, spends a whole morning with us. At every intersection the car stalls and he has to connect two wires under the steering wheel to bring it back to life. Tyeb finds us a computer shop. Worryingly our computer has shut down. Despite the willingness and helpfulness of the staff, after a couple of hours we realize that they are unable to work out the problem. We leave with forbidding visions of having lost the latest photos, GPS maps and whatever else has not been backed up. Later that evening Brian resets the operating system to an earlier version, and the computer starts up.

We visit Ozone, a recommended western-style coffee shop and restaurant, which is yearned for by this time. And finally Tyeb drives us to a tiny supermarket, a welcome excursion, and it is great fun to search the crowded shelves crammed with cans and bottles of unfamiliar brands and labels written in Arabic.

From the 17th floor of the luxury Burj Al-Fateh Hotel there is an expansive view of the confluence of the two Niles – the Blue Nile from Ethiopia and the White Nile from Lake Victoria in Kenya, both of which we have sighted on the way. We treat ourselves to an expensive afternoon tea with the choice of a wide selection of cakes and mouth-watering delicacies. This hotel is way above our budget and caters for high-flying visitors to Khartoum.

As passengers in taxis for a few days, we find we quickly learn the Arabic numerals – very handy when you want to know the real prices for market goods. Number plates have the local Arabic numerals with our familiar Hindu-Arabic digits underneath, so learning them is made easy, and we can both now read and write them – only to 10 though. And after three days in Khartoum we now know *shukran jazeelan* – thank you very much.

★★★

Sudan evokes stories of violence and war, but we are well north of the conflict in Darfur and the people prove to be warm and friendly. A huge wind whips up a sandstorm the day we leave Khartoum as we travel north and follow the Nile, which is not visible from the road. Through the dust and sand of a windy day, we see the pyramids emerging in the distance, little peaks nestled into a rise not far from the road. We are 200 kilometers north of Khartoum and these are the Meroe Pyramids of Sudan from about the third century BC, later than the pyramids of Giza. It is an ancient burial site of the Kingdom of Kush, which at its peak controlled most of the Nile Valley. Over forty kings and queens are buried here, and although many of the pyramids are in ruins, plundered since ancient times, in the isolation of this desert landscape they are impressive. Having set up camp in the classic desert landscape surrounding us, out of sight of the road and the pyramids, we wander over to them in the fading evening light. There is no one around, we have the whole place to ourselves, and there is a sunset haze – it feels magical.

Waking up next morning, we are greeted by four local men swathed in headscarves and robes, jackets over the top for warmth from the early morning desert chill. A camel and two donkeys rest alongside and they have arranged a few artifacts and locally made crafts in a row in the red sand. They have ancient looking knives and sabers, and trinkets and we nod and greet them and a few of us buy. After breakfast we have another wander through the pyramids, this time purchasing an entrance ticket, and the only other visitors are from an Iranian film crew.

This is the country of the Nubian people, which stretches through the desert to Wadi Halfa and Lake Nasser on the border with Egypt. The road is straight, and littered with blown-out tires from the constant stream of trucks that travel up to Port Sudan. The roadblocks are once again prolific, but George has made sure we have all the necessary travel permits and that we have registered with the police, so they are all hassle free and we are welcomed to Sudan with huge smiles and great enthusiasm for Australia, nearly as good as Sudan we are told, and we decide it is not the time to argue the point.

Karima is another 200 kilometers further on and just out of town stands the small flat-topped very small mountain of Jabal Barkal, a landmark for early traders. Standing below are pyramids and the ruins of the Temple of Amun, and in the middle of this hot, barren desert it can be hard to imagine the ancient world that existed here.

We bush camp in the desert again just north of Karima, surrounded by huge logs of petrified wood poking out of the soft sand, before setting off on another day's drive through the stark, bare but beautiful Nubian Desert, an arid expanse of sandstone and sand with little vegetation. We cross a huge bridge across the Nile into Dongola where we refuel and buy fruit and vegetables. From here the road closely follows the Nile as it snakes its way through the sandy desert landscape, dotted with baked brick dwellings. In stark contrast, there are frequent narrow strips of small plots of lush green irrigated crops, and the only trees are scattered date palms. Water can work its wonders even in sand

and clay, or perhaps they use fertilizer.

Our next desert camp is right on the Nile just south of Abri. A few Nubian fishermen wander by, intrigued but they are untroubled by our visit. After three nights of desert camps, with cold nights and not so hot days which has been a pleasant surprise, we reach Wadi Halfa where we are to catch a ferry across Lake Nasser to Egypt, while our vehicles will go separately on a barge.

Since Khartoum, we have been in touch with a fixer, Mazar Mahir who lives in Wadi Halfa and spends much of his time helping travelers negotiate the border crossing out of Sudan, a minefield without some local knowledge. His name was given to us by other overlanders. The ferry and barge are booked, but it is only on arrival that you truly know and understand the whole situation. We meet Mazar who is a delight and very hospitable. He offers us refreshment, tea or a soft drink, in his little shop which serves as his office, a room with a small desk and a few chairs with a large sliding door onto the street, and he gathers our paperwork and tells us of the plan so far. He cannot be sure yet which day the vehicles will leave on the barge, perhaps tomorrow, so we will need to phone him in the morning to confirm. Today is Sunday and the passenger ferry as we already know is leaving on Wednesday. Mazar warns us there is a chance we will not get cabins on board, so we resign ourselves to sleeping on the deck. Before we leave town he suggests we take our lunch to eat inside the garden wall of his house. Wadi Halfa comprises dusty roads through an assortment of walled houses, and on arrival at his home Mazar clears a space for us around a little table under a shaded terrace amongst the desert plants of his garden. His family peek out at us now and then, and smile, and we feel comfortably relaxed in his humble, pleasant garden.

Uninspired by the hotels we camp a few kilometers south of town, feeling dwarfed by the surrounding desert. Dinner is a makeshift affair – we are pooling our food supplies in readiness for empty fridges for the barge trip ahead. Later in the evening after a desert sunset, the night air is crisp and so are the stars, bright and dazzling in the dark desert sky.

We pack up ready to leave next morning with chairs and sleeping bags to take on deck to make ourselves more comfortable on the night-time crossing, as well as food and drinks. We wait for Mazar's phone call and he tells us the barge is now leaving the same day as the ferry which is in two days' time. This is good news. If we leave the same time as our vehicles there will be no need for hotel accommodation in Wadi Halfa. While we wait for our departure we have two more relaxing nights camping in the desert, giving us time to prepare for our night on the deck. There are trips into town for fresh pita bread and tomatoes, and we spend the days relaxing out in the desert, luckily in cool pleasant weather. We cook scones and Bob cooks a couple of great evening meals with our assortment of ingredients.

On the day of departure, we follow Mazar from his shop in a *bajaj* to the terminal where we wait for the customs officials to have their breakfast. Mazar has done a sterling job of finalizing all the paper work for the vehicles. With our gear for the ferry unloaded, Brian, Bob and Dickie take the vehicles to load onto the barge, a test of their driving skills driving down two planks from the wharf to the barge. More waiting and lunch is a banana squashed into fresh pita bread, until we follow Mazar with all our paperwork and passports as he pushes through the crowd to Immigration. Mazar pushes us back through the crowd again, quite mad with people shouting at each other and everyone in a mini panic. In a frenzied hurry we squash onto a bus to the ferry. Once on board, Mazar finds us a great spot on the deck before we shake hands with lots of "*shukran jazeelan*" and he is gone. Shortly afterwards, the ferry is grinding away from the terminal. It is late afternoon and we settle in for the next 18 hours, due to arrive in Aswan some time tomorrow morning. The barge with the vehicles on board has left before us, but soon we see it across the lake and it is very soon behind the ferry and out of sight.

There is a 'call to prayer' followed by a large group of men praying on the deck close by, and another spectacular sunset over the lake with a backdrop of desert landscape, and at approximately this time we steam across the border somewhere beneath the water. We eat our own food we have brought with us, deciding not to risk the food available on our meal tickets, and settle down into our sleeping bags for the night, very snug and comfortable despite the flat hard deck underneath. The engine of the boat is just purring and there is no sensation of moving as we look up at the stars. Early in the night we hear a rumbling of people murmuring and we sit up to see a vision of the Abu Simbel Temples drifting past, the Great Temple of Ramses II with its four colossal seated statues of the pharaoh looking out over the lake, and the Temple of Hathor, fronted by six ten meter high standing statues of Ramses and Nefertari, spectacularly floodlit in a golden hue against the night sky. With a wave of excitement, we know we are in Egypt.

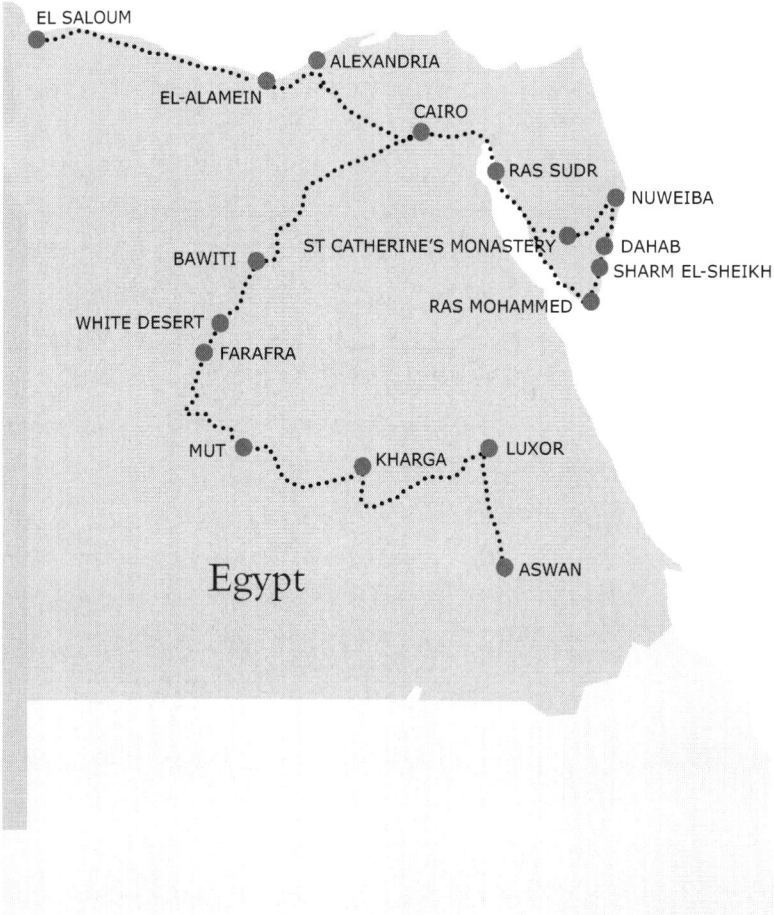

18.

Egypt – baksheesh, Nile feluccas, sphinxes, Tutankhamen and El Alamein remembers

Our introduction to Egyptian soil in Aswan the next morning is in complete contrast to the calm and pleasant evening we have spent on Lake Nasser where during the night we crossed the Tropic of Cancer. An early sunrise and a 'call to prayer' are followed by a simple breakfast before the ferry pulls up near a bank of steep rocks. No one can disembark until, in their own time, the Egyptian customs and immigration officials arrive on a boat and board the ferry to process all the passengers. It takes three hours. Once completed, there is a crazy push-and-shove rush to disembark, with more jostling and elbowing than is at all comfortable, followed by moving along with the crowd through gateways and doors which can unexpectedly shut in the middle of the crowd with no indication of which doorway to rush and crush through next. We carry all our gear through endless checkpoints for more stamping of passports and documentation, so by the time we eventually find our Egyptian fixer, Kamal, we are almost ready to embrace him, but don't.

Kamal guides us through more officialdom, and rescues Bob when his Leatherman knife is discovered on his belt. Out in the street at last, all eight of us and our gear amazingly fit into Kamal's station-wagon taxi – three right in the back, three in the middle and two in the front with Kamal, and gear under the back seats or piled high on the roof rack. We look just like all the overloaded *matatus* we have seen throughout Africa. Kamal takes us to our hotel that we booked back in Sudan. Down a dark arcade, up the steps to a crowded foyer of noise and mayhem where we are told there are no rooms. "No, there is no reservation." Kamal drives us around a few more hotels until at last we have a room for a few nights at the Isis Hotel.

A sundowner of soft drink is now a thing of the past, and we meet at the bar for our first Egyptian beer to celebrate our successful Lake Nasser ferry crossing. The activity on the Nile is captivating from the bar: the tall majestic sails of the feluccas; the highly decorated open-sided motorized passenger boats with people standing on top; and the larger ferries transporting the locals. All are negotiating their way around each other and between some rocky outcrops in the middle of the river with a backdrop of steep sandy hills on the opposite bank. The sun sets over the river and the feluccas become silhouetted triangles against the twilight sky and we feel ready for the fascination of Egypt.

The fascination of Egypt also includes retrieving our vehicles from customs – a minefield of fascination. Brian, Bob and Dickie are collected by Kamal in his taxi and taken through the back streets to a room full of queues to teller-like windows where documents are signed and stamped and various amounts of money exchanged – an introduction to *baksheesh*.

In Egypt we discover *baksheesh* is just a way of life, a cultural phenomenon that as a tourist is better to accept than to resist as it is not restricted to foreigners. In Muslim countries the giving of alms, *zakat*, to the poor is one of the 'Five Pillars of Islam' and giving allows Muslims to demonstrate their faith to Allah. This practice flows over into *baksheesh* for services rendered, similar to western tipping but it goes much further. It is a show of respect, gratitude and appreciation for any service at all and is also expected to be added to any paid service. And then there is *baksheesh* for the granting of favors. While touring an ancient site, offers will abound to show you a forbidden passageway or the best location for a photo, all in the hope of receiving *baksheesh*. The hardest thing is to have plenty of *piaster* coins or small notes wandering about in your pocket – and small change is difficult to come by.

Signing and stamping of documents continues without respite, until Kamal takes his charges for a ride to pick up the customs official from his house. *Baksheesh* is rolling in front of everyone's eyes. The captain of the barge is at the dock – more *baksheesh*. The vehicles are parked in a secure car park – more *baksheesh*. The customs process from custom official to police to custom official continues – more *baksheesh*. The insurance and registration – more and more *baksheesh* – until it is late afternoon and time to go to the government office to collect the Egyptian number plates for each vehicle which have to be strapped over the existing plates – even more *baksheesh*. Finally, there is the settling of the account with Kamal who has been as solid as a rock and invaluable throughout the whole process and definitely deserves *baksheesh*.

★★★

The Cradle of Civilization is a term that comes to mind as we travel through Egypt with the awe- inspiring remnants of the ancient Egyptian civilization. The Nile Valley and the Nile delta supported thirty-one dynasties of Egyptian kings. It is only later we realize that the Egyptian civilization is considered only one of arguably six early civilizations recognized within the Cradle of Civilization terminology.

Aswan introduces us to the world of bazaars in Egypt – long narrow busy alleyways of vendors and tiny shops with entrances almost obliterated by items dangling from great heights so that all is on display. They sell everything – fruit, vegetables, nuts, spices, dried fruit, bread, kitchenware, hardware, colored fabric, scarves and clothing. Some are more geared to the tourist trade with Egyptian artifacts, brass and copper collectables, leather goods, rugs, and jewelry, including the scarab beetle jewelry and carved scarab beetle stones which are touted as being very lucky. The scarab beetle was important to Ancient Egyptians. They likened its emergence from nowhere to the Sun God Ra who created himself out of nothing, becoming a symbol of regeneration and rebirth. The Sun God Ra was seen to renew the sun every day before pushing it along its course in the sky, the same way the scarab beetle rolls dung into a ball in which to lay its eggs and supply food for the larvae.

The vendors are aggressively full on and in your face, trying to entice you to buy, but along with the hard sell they also have a great sense of humor. "Come in, everything for free – while you look." "Let me help you spend your money. Ah, you don't need help, you have her." "Hassle-free shopping just for you." And everything gets cheaper relative to the distance from the shop as you walk away. Despite their hard-sell attitude, they often joke and laugh as you try to drive down the price, which is all part of the game. We buy Egyptian sandals of camel leather, some great scarves, and Brian is shown how to wear the men's checked headscarf 'Egyptian style'. And finally a camel-leather pouf or footrest, just like the one Brian's Uncle Ron brought back from Egypt over forty years ago.

The Nubia Museum has a display of objects and monuments of Egyptian Nubia which were collected after the completion of the High Dam at Aswan in the 1960s before they would be lost forever under the waters of Lake Nasser. Even the Abu Simbel Temples we passed on the ferry were dismantled and relocated to higher ground.

★★★

The drive north to Luxor follows the Nile most of the way and having been delayed leaving Aswan, we know we have left too late and ultimately end up breaking Rule 3 yet again. It is dark when we arrive and after a long stressful search we find Rezeiky Camp, a haven in the middle of Luxor with beautiful all-day shade and a wonderful friendly atmosphere with plenty of other overlanders, all very well looked after by owners Tony and Illy. On our first night there is a bus load of people from Sweden staying at the camp, and we are included in a great meal of traditional food as well as some entertainment – a snake handler, belly dancing and a whirling dervish dancer all accompanied by a live band playing traditional music.

Another night we have a noisy chatter-filled evening when twelve motor homes pull in and squeeze their way into every available space. They are all from Italy having traveled in convoy down through Turkey, Syria and Jordan. A French couple from Brittany, camped in their small campervan with their two little daughters, have also driven the same route to Luxor and were planning to drive back to France through Tunisia and Libya, but a diplomatic row has flared again between Libya and Switzerland over an incident back in 2008. Colonel Gaddafi's son and his wife were arrested for allegedly assaulting their servants at a luxury hotel in Geneva and were detained for two days before being released. So now Gaddafi has banned the issuing of visas to citizens from any Schengen country. The Schengen Area of Europe includes those countries which have abolished passport and immigration controls at their common borders resulting in the whole area functioning as a single country for international travel purposes. Fortunately, Australians are not included in the ban, nor are travelers from the UK, but the French couple is madly trying to come up with an alternative. Shipping from Alexandria is expensive as their vehicle does not fit into a shipping container so it seems they will have to drive back the way they have come.

Egyptian food is often a variation of traditional Middle Eastern food. In Aswan we have our first taste of Egyptian cuisine – 'Beef *Tagen* Nubian-style and Shish Kebab Lamb. *Tagen* is a tasty stew served piping hot in little earthenware pots. At Rezeiky Camp which is a family enterprise, the women cook traditional food at the outdoor café most nights and it is delicious and very cheap. In Luxor we eat in many restaurants along the Nile. We taste *kofta* (ball-shaped lamb or beef peppered with spices) and *Mahalabiyya*, an Egyptian pudding mixture of rice, milk and sugar. Most meals finish with at least a small piece of sweet cake. One evening walking home after a restaurant meal, we hear drums and tambourines, singing and clapping, and first one, then another wedding couple emerge onto the street, the white dresses of the brides massed with jewels. They are followed by their happy guests who crowd round each bride and groom, and then the newlywed couples leave in waiting cars.

Luxor is a tourist mecca. Dozens of Nile cruisers nestle into the corniche along the river at night, in long rows, three or four deep, and dozens of tourist coaches add to the chaos of the streets. So the tourist sites in Luxor are best seen early in the cool of the morning and before the masses of tourist buses arrive. There is so much in Luxor to draw tourists from all over the world. The Avenue of Sphinxes lines the entrance to the Karnak Temple and on another day on a walk back from the markets we see an excavation in progress to reveal more ram-headed sphinxes. There were once 1350 of them along the 70 meter wide avenue which extends to the Luxor Temple, 2 to 3 kilometers away.

In the Great Hypostyle Hall at Karnak, 134 columns stand in 16 rows where once they supported a roof. Now they are towering massive monuments and as you wander through the columns they loom above and completely surround you like a huge maze. When I lose Brian for a short while, it feels a lot worse than losing him in the supermarket.

Back in Aswan walking along the corniche, we browsed through a bookshop with a wealth of information on iconic ancient Egyptian architecture in the Nile Valley. We couldn't help purchasing a little book called *Egypt Then and Now*, an illustrated guide with a colored overlay for each present-day photograph showing the forms and colors that may have been part of the original appearance. Now as we visit these ancient monuments these images help us to visualize their past magnificence.

In the limestone hills on the west bank of the Nile is the Valley of the Kings which contains 63 tombs and chambers of Egyptian royals from the New Kingdom between the 16th and 11th Centuries BC. An entry ticket only permits a visit to three tombs which can be chosen from images on a computer at the entrance. We choose Siptah (KV47), Ramses I (KV16) and Taousert/Setnakhte which is a double burial site (KV14). They are all different and worth every minute. So many encyclopedia photos are suddenly real and meters away, and some of the decorations in the tombs and in the hieroglyphics still vibrant with color.

Luxor Temple is overwhelming in its grand style, massive columns and statues that have weathered the centuries, though there were thousands of years when the temple was buried below the streets and houses of Luxor. Lit up at night it is an awesome sight. The Romans constructed a military fort around it that the Arabs later called *Al-Uqsur* (the Fortifications) giving modern Luxor its name. Luxor Museum expands on all we have seen so far, a collection of quality pieces in an uncluttered display, and the Cachette Hall was built most recently to house a number of excellent statues found near Luxor Temple in 1987. We top off our Luxor experience with a boat ride up the Nile, perfectly timed for the sunset.

In Luxor we receive a parcel from home which Paul has sent by DHL. It contains a gas regulator. We have been managing without our gas stove since Lalibela in Ethiopia – our jiko has come in handy. Paul posted the regulator on a Thursday afternoon in Sydney and it arrives in Luxor on Sunday morning. We are cooking with gas again!

From Luxor we travel on our own again, as Dickie and Claire and Bob and Maria have different time frames for the rest of the journey to Europe. So we say our goodbyes to our travel companions of the last six weeks. We have so enjoyed our time together, and gone places we wouldn't have gone alone. Wonderful people, wonderful company and we hope we will meet up again someday, maybe somewhere in Europe or England.

★★★

The Western Desert stretches west from the Red Sea over a vast area to the border with Libya where it becomes the Libyan Desert. There are two direct routes to Cairo from Luxor, one along a tarred road following the Nile and another on a road along the Red Sea and the Gulf of Suez. But we have heard from other overlanders along the way about a different option through the Western Desert which is worth the wide detour to Cairo and the extra kilometers.

A string of large oases punctuates the vast stretches of the Western Desert. Almost magically, the water found under these depressions in the desert floor materializes into huge islands of startling green crops, date palms, and towns or cities of people where there had been none, all emerging out of the surrounding glare of the wide and barren desert sand. With four roadblocks along the way, our first stop is 230 kilometers from Luxor in the Kharga Oasis at El Kharga which lies on an ancient trade route but is now a modern fast growing city where the government is encouraging settlement through its New Valley Project. We camp in the grounds of the Kharga Oasis Hotel, a concrete structure surrounded by a neglected palm-filled garden on a busy road of horn-honking traffic, but we are well looked after by the hotel staff who even sell us some fresh pita bread.

Along the road to Dakhla Oasis we start noticing the roadside desert-style 'picnic areas' – huge cement structures on the side of the road to provide shade. They look weird but must be precious relief at times from the stark baked landscape. One time we pull up to have a closer look and take a photograph, but how silly do we feel when the vehicle gets sand bogged in a small section of pure sand between the tarred road and the cement under the shelter. We lower the pressure in all the tires, and shovel away some of the sand around our track, and Brian is just about to hop in to try again, when a carload of Egyptian men stop to help. Before we know it one fellow has sat himself in the driver's seat, started up the engine and driven out, no doubt wondering what the hell has been our problem. We can only laugh with them all and enjoy the self-satisfied look on the hero's face as we wave them off and turn around to re-inflate the tires. And take the photo.

In the town of Mut in the Dakhla Oasis we find the El-Dohous Village Hotel, also called the Bedouin Camp, a highly decorated mud brick structure with a desert garden strewn with decorative rocks, but with no shade in the campground so we take a moderately priced room. Nearby is Al-Qasr where we organize a guided walking tour of a medieval Ottoman town. Beneath pink limestone hills on the edge of the Dakhla Oasis, it is an intriguing rabbit warren of two and three storey mud houses and narrow alleyways, weathered but still defiantly revealing its history.

The White Desert is famous for its brilliant white limestone formations that are the remains of microscopic marine animals deposited 80 million years ago. The harsh winds in the desert have sculptured these formations into unusual shapes which in the normal beautiful sunshine look surreal – apparently! We are stopped by a police roadblock as we attempt to leave Farafra for the White Desert drive. The wind has blown up suddenly and within minutes we are in the middle of a sandstorm, with visibility like a pea-soup fog. The police for our own safety will not let us through. We head back to a motel we have just driven past, thinking that camping in the midst of a sandstorm might not be too pleasant. The wind is whipping up the sand even within the walls that surround the motel, but whether it is from this sandstorm or from a dozen or so before it, the rooms have more sand in them than they could possibly clean up in the "It will only take five minutes!" time frame that they promise. We camp in our sand-free camper, but the wind howls and the camper flaps around us entire night, yet we still wake up sand free. Visibility is still poor the next morning but the police let us through. Our White Desert experience, however, is a beige one, shrouded in nature's windy onslaught of sand. What can you do? That's travel – take it as you find it on the day – and we did experience a full-on sandstorm!

We contact Omar, the Egyptian from Alexandria whom we met back in Tanzania. Omar runs tour groups through the White Desert. We meet him at a campsite near Bawiti. He is a typically tricky Egyptian and when we inquire about inspections of vehicles for registration, he offers to 'inspect' our car on the spot, with the help of his brother who is here, and by chance an excellent mechanic. They have already detected broken springs which they say definitely need replacing right now. We are not convinced. We decline his offer, as well as the offer of a tour back through that questionably white White Desert the next day. Instead we enjoy a Bedouin meal and Omar's company around a Bedouin camp fire with Bedouin music and enthusiastic clapping.

On our last day in the Western Desert, 30,000 kilometers roll over on the odometer for our journey so far and it's exciting to be heading to Cairo, rather a milestone and so close to the Mediterranean and Europe. The excitement is short-lived with the reality of Cairo traffic and wrong turns and arguments with the GPS while we search for our campsite in the congested city suburb of Giza, home of the Pyramids.

★★★

Salma Camp in Giza is another city haven for overlanders. Only a five minute walk away, taxis into the center of Cairo are quite cheap, though on the first day we fall victim to the very obliging and friendly taxi driver who hangs about the campsite – and charges almost double. From up in our camper we can see one of the pyramids out the window, and five times a day the 'call to prayer' is an intriguing chorus from all the surrounding mosques. Tom and Jemma from England are our camp neighbors for the week, as their trip south is delayed while they wait for parts for their vehicle to be shipped to Cairo. We meet Nico and Melody who are driving from the Netherlands to Singapore.

It is in Cairo that our Libyan visa saga begins. We are hoping that the application we submitted in Addis Ababa for a transit visa without the necessity of a guide has been processed and is ready for us to collect. Not even close. We phone a Mr Adam at the Libyan Consulate in Alexandria whose name we have been given. Mr Adam knows nothing about us or any visa application sent from Addis Ababa.

Nico and Melody have driven all through Libya and recommend their guide, Ahmed, who was very good they assure us, despite accidentally crossing the border into Algeria in the middle of the Libyan Desert by mistake, and getting himself into a fix with the authorities. We call Ahmed but our vehicle without a passenger seat for the guide is just too hard for him. Tom and Jemma have just come across with a Libyan guide too but they found their five days with the guide very expensive. So a transit visa without a guide is still our preferred option, and we have been led to believe this is possible. Our other option is to travel through Jordan and Syria and into Turkey, but having reached Cairo we are feeling travel weary and eager to start the journey home for a break. We know we would not do justice to a much longer drive through more countries.

The Libyan Embassy in Cairo is our next line of attack. After the first of many taxi rides to the embassy, we arrive to find the embassy is closed on Tuesdays. It is also closed on Fridays for 'Prayer Day', a religious holy day and nor does it open on Sundays. So we catch a taxi into the center of Cairo to Tahrir Square and spend much of the day at the Egyptian Museum. It is so huge and impressive and we wander through a maze of rooms and halls bursting with antiquities. There is way too much to see and we try an organized approach, having selected certain rooms from the guidebook that are must-see. But distractions are many along the way and getting lost is easy. The Tutankhamun Gallery is a huge highlight, housing hundreds of beautifully preserved artifacts from the 1922 archaeological find of Tutankhamun's tomb filled with all the king would need in his afterlife. The spectacular golden funerary mask glows in a darkened room and is unbelievably right there in front of us.

The following day our visit to the Libyan Embassy is challenging. Yesterday the street was practically empty, but today a large crowd has gathered outside, stretching across the road making life difficult for any traffic. They are men and mostly young, all waiting to get into the visa office. We find out from a guard at a gate around the corner that the visa office will not open until ten o'clock. It is now 8.45 am. Feeling rather overwhelmed by the situation around us, we wonder how we will manage to get inside. We wait across the road watching children playing in a schoolyard which backs on to the street, the noise so typical of a playground anywhere.

When the doors finally open, the crowd swarms towards the man at the door who shouts at them, and chooses the few who can enter. We stand back a little, and to our surprise the man at the door soon spots us and motions for us to come forward. The crowd lets us squeeze through and we are inside a gloomy room divided by a glass screen which is shielding desks where a couple of officials take their time to start processing those lucky enough to be inside. We are told to sit on a couple of the chairs lining the edge of the room and we watch the comings and goings for quite some time. The doors only re-open when there are enough people waiting to get back outside, and the crowd then surges making it difficult for those trying to leave. A burly, well dressed young man is on door duty and yells to gain control. He chooses the next lucky dozen or so who can now enter. We wait patiently on our chairs and chat to a fellow next to us who explains that most of the young men are applying for visas to work in Libya. He is himself a labor contractor. Another man tells us he is a doctor from Iraq trying to get a work visa into Libya. He hopes to work in Europe one day. Meanwhile, we notice a couple of those still waiting outside passing their documents in through the one and only barred window to friends or relatives. There must be fewer jobs than there are Egyptians prepared to pack up and work over the border. There is a sense of desperation which makes our mission seem so trivial.

Eventually we are summoned and given a form to fill in. We hand in the form, sit down and wait until we are called again to fill in another form – we apparently need one each! More waiting until we are told of the other requirements – the Arabic translation in the back of our passports (tick), the myriad of photocopies of all our documents (tick). We pass them through the hole in the glass screen. It is so difficult to talk through glass with noise in the room behind us. We are told it will take a minimum of two weeks for our application to be sent to Tripoli in Libya to be processed and returned, and Sameh (pronounced Shamere), who appears to be the most senior, hands us his phone number to call in two weeks time. We then wait our turn to be cast out through the door with others to the chaos outside, and find a taxi to take us back to Giza.

Gathering our thoughts back at Salma Camp, we decide we can handle the two week wait as long as we are not worried about our period of stay expiring on our Egyptian visa. We can have a leisurely trip to the Sinai and relax on the Red Sea for the next couple of weeks while we wait. The Salma Camp owner advises us we can apply for an extension on our visa at the Ministry of Foreign Affairs. To start off the process straight away we get another taxi back to Tahrir Square which is near the Ministry's address we have located on the internet. A kind Egyptian on the steps of the building offers his help and points to a different building across the square and after many more enquiries we find the right building and the right floor and the right area and the right counter and the right window, and we are handed forms to take away and fill in and bring back tomorrow. We complete them there and then only to be told. "No, nine o'clock tomorrow bring them back". *Mmmm.* We console ourselves with two very expensive beers at the Intercontinental where the café and bar overlook the Nile, before catching another taxi back to our camp, but not one of the many taxis waiting outside the hotel because they charge a premium. It has been a huge day and with exhaustion settling in it definitely feels like a why-are-we-doing-this sort of day.

The next morning we are back at the Ministry at 8.45 am, brimming with the confidence of knowing where to go. We wait at Window 12, only to be told at nine o'clock that we need to go to a different window to buy stamps for our forms. By now queues have formed but the time passes quickly. We are intrigued by the diversity of skin color, dress and culture gathered in one place. There are people from all parts of the world and everyone is on a mission for permission to leave or stay in Egypt. Back to Window 12 with our stamps secure on our forms, we hand them over the counter with our passports and are informed we must go to Window 38 in two hours time to pick up our visas. We spend the time back at the Intercontinental sipping expensive coffees watching the hazy Nile River alive with activity, and dignitaries arriving and departing the hotel in their black Mercedes Benz cars shadowed by security guards. They are probably just going to the Arab League Headquarters across from the hotel.

Back at Window 38 quite a crowd has gathered, similarly waiting for their papers or passports. Brian has his within half an hour, mine takes two hours. We are concerned and confused by the wait, but at last both passports are in our hands, and they have extended our period of stay to six months! "A temporary residence for touristic purposes" it says, so Brian thinks we should get an apartment in Cairo – I don't think so!

But that is not the end of it. Yesterday Brian had confirmation from Window 12 that we will also have to extend our vehicle carnet at the Ministry of Traffic, and the man even wrote the address in Arabic on a piece of paper for us. We have no idea where it is located, but taxis are cheap, especially the beaten-up black taxis with drivers who will negotiate a price before the journey. Jumping through all these bureaucratic hoops is now a priority. Tomorrow is Prayer Day so we are prepared to forgo an afternoon to ensure our vehicle also enjoys an extended stay in Egypt, though we doubt we will achieve as much today.

We hand the address to the driver and at faster than normal breakneck speed through the Cairo traffic he takes off. He is wild. Middle Eastern music blares from his radio, beads and air fresheners sway from the rear view mirror, and he toots endlessly at nothing in particular or at the car ahead when the traffic is jammed. Suddenly we are out on the freeways and we begin to wonder just where we might end up. *Surely the Ministry of Traffic* isn't way out here? But Cairo is a huge city, and sure enough, after twenty minutes he drops us outside a drab building. We manage to convey to people lingering outside just what we are looking for. They point upstairs and we find the right floor and the right room and the right window and within ten minutes

Bruno has an extended stay for a minimal fee. We are shocked. It has happened so fast that we are not convinced. We ask a well dressed local employee walking past if he can read Arabic. He checks our paperwork and nods. Yes, even our vehicle can stay for six months!

★★★

Egyptian pita bread becomes our all time favorite. A short stroll from Salma Camp is a tiny bakery where we buy fresh pita bread every day. It rolls out on a wire grill from the five hundred degree hot oven, puffed up like a flying saucer, before it collapses as it cools. And it is really cheap.

We have heard from other overlanders on our way north through Egypt that a surprise awaits us when we reach Cairo – a huge Carrefour supermarket within a western-style mall. Our last supermarket was in Khartoum, so we have been looking forward to this one, a very exciting prospect in these circumstances. All the goodies that we have easily managed without, but which now seem essential, are there for the asking. By this stage we are also craving a real coffee, a flat white or a cappuccino, and it is all there waiting for us in multiple coffee shops and western coffee chains.

With all our cheap city tours in taxis we see more of Cairo than we had thought possible – it's so huge and ramshackle with tall unfinished and rather unattractive apartments adorned with washing and satellite discs. From the 'comfort' of our taxis, we conclude that Cairo traffic is insanely organized chaos and bedlam, but it actually works. Driving within lane boundaries is obviously a waste of time and a waste of precious space on the roads – four lanes can easily become seven. Where a car can fit, a car will go. One day we have the added bonus of one of our taxi drivers asking directions from another taxi driver as we all drive along at a speed a little too fast for such a conversation.

As pedestrians we discover we are also in dangerous territory, but we shadow the locals with much less confidence as they attempt to wave the traffic to slow down when vehicles career towards them. For lunch we enjoy some traditional food in the city which we think is cheap until we pay the service fees and taxes. We need a break from Cairo. We leave on a Friday Prayer Day with much less traffic throughout the city – a good start for our trip across to the Sinai Peninsula. But we cannot leave before we have visited the Great Pyramids of Giza.

An early morning start puts us first in line at the ticket office windows and before 8 am we are striding through the Giza Necropolis in the cool of the morning. It is impossible not to be transfixed by the sight of these massive ancient monuments. Even just the building blocks of the Pyramid of Khufu are taller than Brian. The tomb of Queen Hetepheres is a collapsed and much smaller pyramid. Brian starts the climb down the dark deep shaft to the burial chamber just as one of the workers runs over to turn on the lights – it makes quite a difference and quickly resolves my momentary indecision to follow. Having climbed down about 25 meters, we get a claustrophobic feel for what the pyramids are like inside. Back outside, excitement soars with the sight of the Great Sphinx of Giza as it gazes across the haze of the sprawling city of Cairo, where it has gazed for over four thousand years and has seen infinitely more than the imagination can even summon.

★★★

It is good to be out of busy, bustling Cairo and on the hectic highway towards Sinai, where in no time the drab urban landscape changes to one of desert with occasional apartment complexes in the middle of nowhere. We are heading for the Suez Tunnel – just another tunnel – but definitely a different experience if you are lucky enough to sight a ship seemingly cruising through the desert, visible only from about the deck upwards, and then silently gliding above the entrance to the tunnel as you descend beneath the canal.

We drive down the barren but beautiful western coastline of the Sinai Peninsula along the Gulf of Suez towards Ras Sudr. Strewn alongside the beaches are countless resorts many of which look either uninhabited or only half built, but always with huge and elaborate gated entrances.

The Sinai Stars Resort is well beyond its past glory days of perhaps five star rating. We enter a spacious marbled reception area which is covered in a fine layer of sand. No one is around until a lone employee appears who is happy to show us a room overlooking the beach. There are obviously no other guests and it is the off season so we feel the room rate is a little high and enquire about camping within the resort complex. This we can do at a very reasonable rate right on the beach. It is quite a strange experience, but we feel completely safe despite the fact that all around us is a 'ghost resort'. It must have once been very luxurious with swimming pool, bar on the beach, thatched umbrellas, beach chairs, but all in complete disarray now. We learn later the resorts were once frequented by Israeli and European holidaymakers but many tourists have stopped coming to the Sinai for holidays since the unrest of the 90s and more recent events. We also learn that there was a devastating storm about six weeks ago which came in from the Red Sea, washed away sand and inflicted a good deal of damage along the coast. This accounts for the mayhem of up-ended thatched umbrellas and smashed outdoor furniture along the beach.

St Catherine's Monastery is inland on the way to the eastern coast. We camp nearby, but the Monastery is closed so we are unable to explore inside. Feeling unfit after months of car travel and too little exercise, and one of us with a head cold, we decide not to climb Mount Sinai – so this has not been a hugely successful visit. Despite this we enjoy getting a feel for this biblical site which is of huge significance to Judaism, Christianity and Islam. This part of Sinai has a spectacular rocky desert landscape which can appear red, orange, brown or pink, depending on the light, and it defies comprehension of the hardships suffered by all those who have made the long and arduous pilgrimage for so many centuries.

In the little village below the monastery, Brian rushes into the bakery to buy pita bread just as we are leaving, and runs back out juggling the super hot bread which has just come out of the oven. The hot bread is juggled back and forth between us until we eventually manage to locate a bag for it.

We spend four nights on the eastern Sinai coast at Nuweiba where the ferry leaves for Jordan. We find a very reasonably priced resort, which does have other guests! It is situated right on the beach looking out over the Gulf of Aquaba, and on a clear day we can see Saudi Arabia. It is warm enough for good swimming and relaxing on the beach.

Further south Dahab is a popular Red Sea diving destination, with plenty of tourists, but far more appealing is Ras Mohammad

National Park on the very southern tip of the Sinai Peninsula. The campsite is meters from the water on a tiny alcove of a beach which we share with Marguerita from Norway and Frederik from Germany who have just driven down through Turkey, Syria and Jordan. On the very first afternoon we discover that snorkeling just a few strokes into the water reveals beautiful bright colored coral and huge numbers of colored fish – and the biggest parrot fish we have ever seen. There are very few people around and we thoroughly enjoy the luxury of snorkeling off the beach at our leisure, glad we brought our snorkeling gear which has spent most of the time gathering dust in one of the back drawers. We have only brought the snorkeling masks and snorkel, thinking fins are easy enough to hire and would take up too much room in the camper. But no fins to hire here!

After Marguerita and Frederik leave, we spend one night on our own, and for two nights have the company of two fellow Aussie campers from Melbourne who are driving south from England. We meet some friendly locals, a Bedouin with a European wife on a camping weekend with their children, and another Egyptian who is a diving instructor and whose wife is from Denmark. On the last day when it is windy and not suitable for snorkeling, we explore Sharm el-Sheikh which is so full of resorts and tourists that we soon retreat back to our campsite at Ras Mohammad.

When we ring the Libyan Embassy in Cairo we are told there is no information about our visas, and that we should phone again in a few days. We decide to travel back to Cairo to visit the Embassy in person, which will be just over two weeks since we applied for the visas. We also email shipping companies to enquire about the cost of shipping our vehicle from Alexandria to Marseilles in France. The cost is not prohibitive, but when we do our sums and add the cost of our flights and accommodation at either end while the vehicle is on the Mediterranean, it becomes very expensive.

Moon Beach Resort, on the way back up the coast towards Ras Sudr, is known as a perfect kite surfing destination on this windy coastal location. We get a very reasonably priced room, and once again see the results of the huge storm that hit this coast a few weeks earlier. Hoping for some great photos of the ships passing through the canal, we visit Suez but there is to be no ship for two hours, so we continue on to Cairo and Salma Camp at Giza once again. Our relaxed Sinai visit has been a stark contrast to the traffic and city bustle and rush that is Cairo.

With a day to spare before we run the gauntlet of the Libyan Embassy again, we catch yet another taxi into the city to spend some time in the souk of Khan al-Khalili, a market which sells everything to anybody, both locals and tourists. It is a labyrinth of narrow alleyways and courtyards and easily confuses, but we find Fishawi's Coffeehouse, an institution which claims to have been serving coffee for 200 years, with mirrored walls and traditional decor combined with the aromas of the strong coffee and the *sheesha* (water pipe) smoking all adding to the intrigue. A traditional lunchtime meal at the Gad Restaurant completes a great day in the Egyptian capital.

Much to our disappointment, after the obligatory and arduous waiting in the same very crowded, noisy room full of locals applying for visas to work in Libya, we are eventually told that once again there is no information regarding our visa application, and that we should come back on Tuesday (today is Thursday). By now we have decided our preferred route to Europe is definitely through Libya and Tunisia, which was our original plan, so we try very hard to remain optimistic – admittedly through gritted teeth. Alexandria is still to be experienced and not too far away for us to return to Cairo afterwards and hopefully pick up our Libyan visas.

★★★

We find the hotel recommended to us by Liz and Peter, and it is called ... The Egypt Hotel. It occupies just the third floor of an Edwardian building. A little box-like open French-style lift of polished timber with a grilled door creaks its way up to our room. We have a tiny balcony which overlooks the corniche and the Mediterranean Sea and here for the first time we suddenly have a sense of having driven the full length of the African continent. Just over that sparkling expanse of water is Turkey and we feel very close to Europe.

The Egypt Hotel makes our stay in Alexandria near perfect. It is very reasonably priced and breakfast is included – a plate with slices of tomato, cheese, Devon-type meat, cucumber, and olives, as well as butter and jam and fresh bread, and Nescafe coffee is there for the asking. The hotel is in an ideal location, just two small blocks from the Midan Saad Zaghloul, the most elegant square on Alexandria's Corniche. Here once stood the Caesareum, where Cleopatra committed suicide in 30 BC. The two giant obelisks known as Cleopatra's needles which used to stand in front of the temple were moved in 1877, one to the Thames embankment in London and the other to Central Park in New York.

The Cecil Hotel is also on the square, built in 1929 and

oozing old world charm and elegance which complements an expensive light lunch. In the vicinity we also discover some even better coffee houses and pastry shops, including Athineos which has been open since 1900, and still has its 1940s fittings and period character with mirrors, timber furniture and paneled walls, and spectacular light fittings, not to mention its selection of traditional biscuits baked on the premises.

By this time we are finding Turkish coffee very palatable because cappuccinos can be random in this part of the world. But our favorite coffee retreat is Fayoumi's where fresh sweet local delicacies are available every day to accompany the bitter taste of the coffee, and so cheap. We buy a warm jacket for Brian advertised in a shop window at a special price. Had we not known our Arabic numerals we might have paid the premium the shop assistant added to the purchase.

We stay six nights in Alexandria and eat so much seafood. Along with dozens of families and couples, we walk the Corniche at night, twice to our favorite restaurant The Fish Market, popular with the locals and overlooking the lights of the coastline. A wood fired oven delivers freshly cooked pita bread which is served with hummus and at least five other accompanying spreads as an entree. Your seafood meal is chosen from the display on ice, and the chef enquires as to how you might like it cooked, suggesting politely that grilled will release the superb flavors. He is right.

Our other favorite eating place for lunch or dinner is Taverna, where from the upstairs restaurant you can view one of the chefs expertly throwing the dough in the sidewalk kitchen below to keep up with the constant orders from the passing pedestrian traffic, and slicing off shavings of *shawarma* (meat on a vertical spit) and serving it as a pita bread sandwich. We also watch him fill thin dough with sweet or savory filling and wrap it all up into a square envelope before sliding it into the open oven, and we wonder what this is called. On asking we are told that this is a 'bai', which we dutifully try to remember, only to laugh at ourselves later when we realize he was merely saying pie, but of course different to the pie we know at home, and actually on the menu as oriental pie. We try one – beautiful light pastry and, of course, we have a seafood filling.

Alexandria is such an interesting and ancient city steeped in history with so many different influences over the centuries. Many antiquities are hidden six meters under the sea as a result of the Crete earthquake of 365 AD and the tsunami which followed and devastated the southern and eastern coasts of the Mediterranean, killing thousands. We are sorry to leave our Egypt Hotel room and our sea-breeze view of the Eastern Harbor, the men, women, couples and families walking the corniche day and night, and the traffic hooting and tooting incessantly in the traffic jam below. As the Athineos menu says, "It's as important to enjoy the atmosphere as it is to see the sights".

On Tuesday we dutifully ring the Libyan Embassy in Cairo, to be told there is still no news of our visas. Disappointment again! Out of frustration we visit the Libyan Consulate in Alexandria and after explaining our three week wait for visas, a very helpful Mr Ahmed phones Sameh in Cairo, and after a long and incomprehensible conversation we are told that our approval has miraculously arrived in Cairo since our earlier phone call. We immediately buy a train ticket to Cairo leaving at 7 am the next morning.

Once again we arrive at the Libyan Embassy to endure the obligatory and arduous waiting in a very crowded, noisy room, but an even longer wait than usual. We are full of apprehension this time, which is justified when 'our friend' Sameh behind the dirty glass screen informs us that yes, our visas have been approved but not processed, and that will take until next Sunday (and today is Wednesday)! Calm, restraint and more patience are mustered from the depths where there is little left to draw from, and we implore Sameh to complete the processing that day as we have come down from Alexandria. He promises he will try though they are very busy. "Come back at one o'clock", he tells us. At 2 pm we have our visas, but rather than feeling elated we feel downtrodden – we had to pay an extra processing fee and if we wanted a receipt that would have taken longer. We are ready to leave Egypt.

★★★

In Alexandria we also have the troubling prospect of Bruno needing to be re-registered. Along the road we have already sent countless emails to RTA NSW, in plenty of time before the due date, asking that they send us the pink slip because we have been unable to download it from their website. Eventually the email arrives but by now it is March, and the vehicle registration is due this month.

RTA NSW has also agreed to our proposal that a Toyota dealership safety inspection will be sufficient for proof of roadworthiness, because the Ministry of Transport in Cairo do not process foreign vehicles. We find the Toyota dealership in Alexandria and all the staff is very obliging and happy to do our safety check right away, though it will take three hours. They offer to drop us off at a small shopping center not too far away while we wait. All goes to plan, though those tricky Egyptians try to nearly double the quote they gave us earlier when it comes time to pay. We protest, so they just agree to the original quote.

They have filled in our precious pink slip, nothing needs to be done to the vehicle, and it is signed by the manager just to make sure. Straight away we email the scanned and completed form to RTA NSW. It is not good enough. By now we are back on the road heading for Libya. Our frustration is paramount. We send more emails but no one wants to take responsibility for this registration because it is out of the comfort zone, in the too hard basket, and easier just to pass it on to the next desk. There is little we can do now. We have no choice but to take the risk and drive through Europe without insurance in an unregistered vehicle. It is a huge risk, but we are at our wits' end. We will sort it out when we get home.

★★★

Despite the frustrations, we continue to enjoy the diversity of all that Egypt has to offer, including the joy of filling up with diesel. One tank of fuel in Alexandria costs AU$12.00 which is only AU$0.22 per liter compared with about AU$1.60 back in Australia.

Driving west from Alexandria we pass ugly, empty-looking apartment buildings plonked onto a dry desert backdrop. There is no sign of the Mediterranean until we get closer to the El Alamein War Museum, situated on the very site of the Battle of El Alamein. Outside, the rusted relics of tanks, trucks, planes and weapons are on display, while inside the complete story of World War II in North Africa is captured in a series of halls, each

dedicated to one of the four countries involved in the war –
Great Britain (including the Ninth Division of the Australian
Imperial Force), Italy, Germany and Egypt. One of the museum
employees proudly demonstrates a model map of North Africa
from Egypt across to Tunisia with tiny model troops and tanks,
and he conducts a little 'light and sound show' wielding his
pointer and manually turning the lights and sound on and off to
reveal all the different battle locations and their tactics.

At El Alamein Commonwealth War Cemetery neat rows
of more than 7000 tombstones dot the sun-baked desert along
with the occasional cactus plants, olive trees and small stands
of purple flowering bougainvillea, encircled by the surrounding
desert scrubland. We find the Australian section, tombstones so
far from their homeland. One of a Private age 35 reads, "HE
HAS FOUGHT THE GOOD FIGHT LOVING HUSBAND
OF IDA" – a poignant reminder of the scale of the tragic loss
here, not only by Australia but other nations remembered in
cemeteries further along the road.

More ugly sentinels of apartment buildings and entrance
gates lie at a distance on the coastal side of the road, emerging
from the barren sand between the huge power lines and plastic
bags and rubbish blowing along in the wind. We see mini buses
full of men and all their bags and belongings piled dangerously
high on top, perhaps a testament to all we have witnessed in the
Libyan Embassy in Cairo.

We spend two nights at an exceptionally beautiful resort, Jaz
Almaza Beach Resort, right on the Mediterranean with highly
visible security cameras and guards. It is out of season with very
few guests. After a welcoming glass of fresh orange juice, we are
told they cannot negotiate a more reasonable price. "Everything

is negotiable in Egypt," quips Brian, which elicits a hearty laugh and a much more reasonable price for dinner, bed and breakfast. It is five-star with the rooms surrounding a mass of swimming pools which lead on to a private beach of rows and rows of blue sun lounges under thatched umbrellas, all empty.

In stark contrast, the following night we stay at a not so nice 'sleeping bag' hotel, with a meager room where a sleeping bag is comforting to throw on top of a rough old rug, the only bedding supplied. We are a short distance from the Libyan border in Saloum, built on pure desert right on the Mediterranean Sea. It is a blustery wind-swept afternoon, and the sand lingers in the sky as it has done all day. We walk along the corniche and find a little bakery to buy some bread but they are sold out. A man standing close by gives us his bread and we try to say thanks but no thanks but he insists, so we try to pay him but he refuses to be paid. We thank him and he seems happy and is on his way.

★★★

The next morning we arrive at the border early, which is just as well. At the first building through the gate we must get the chassis and engine numbers read for a small fee. We still have some Egyptian pounds despite having filled up with fuel before the border, but it doesn't last long. At the second building we pay the next small fee for the vehicle and carnet, and after the next larger fee we need to change some US dollars into Egyptian pounds as they will only take local currency. We have to find the little bank office and by this time we have Mr Mohammed helping us. He had introduced himself at the beginning of this process, and we politely told him we didn't need his help, but now we are finding him useful to direct us to all the different buildings and offices. We are now told to go back to the first building where we have to buy a folder in which to put all the documents we have collected along the way and finally we have to pay to hand over the documents! *Baksheesh, baksheesh.* We are asked for twenty Egyptian pounds and when we say we have only ten left he says, "Okay". Our Egyptian number plates are handed in and we drive a short way to Immigration where we fill in a departure form to hand in with our passport (a standard practice) but we have to buy stamps at a counter in the other corner of the large room. We do have just enough coins left for this and the stamps are now on our departure form. That is the end of our labyrinth of paperwork and bureaucracy to leave Egypt and surprisingly Mr Mohammed is nowhere to be seen for his share of *baksheesh.*

But Libya, here we come at last!

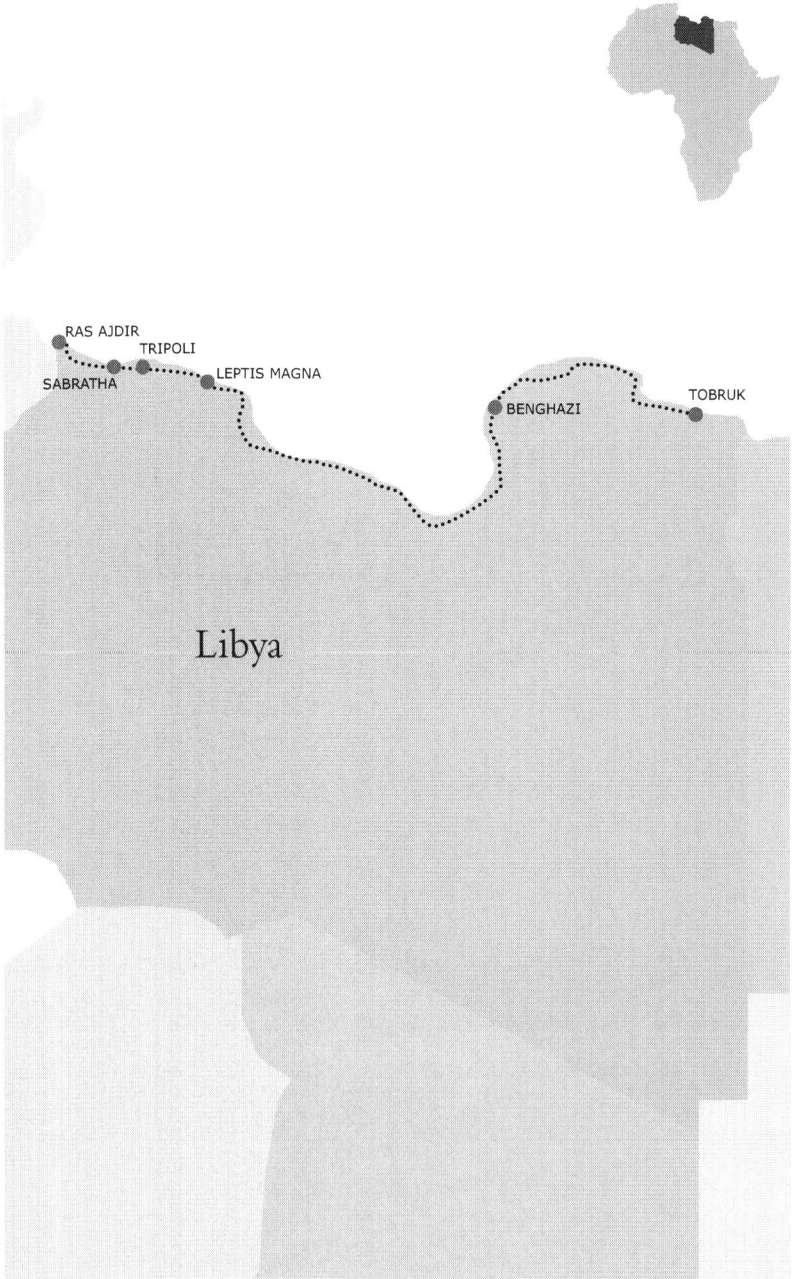

19.

Libya – friendly locals, the Rats of Tobruk and lonely gravestones, lost in Tripoli and simply marbleous ancient ruins

In this part of the world it seems the helpers are just that and expect no payment, and on the Libyan side we are befriended by another very helpful fixer who voluntarily steers us through all the ins and outs of entering Libya. Our passports are stamped quite quickly, but again it is the vehicle that takes time. Our fixer organizes all the paperwork for the license plates and the carnet and helps us find where to change US dollars to Libyan dinars to pay the fees for the license plates. Now we need to hop into a taxi with him for the few kilometers to the border town of Amsaad to physically secure the license plates. The taxi is a beat-up ancient Peugeot with very little lining left inside, totally worn-out seats, door handles that work intermittently and the now familiar engine start-up by connecting the wires under the dashboard, and soon we are parked outside an office waiting for our fixer, who then takes us to another office over the road where we go in and sit down and wait some more. Then back to the first office and we wait in the taxi again until our fixer hops back in with our plates under his arm at last. Throughout the whole exercise the taxi driver has been smiling and friendly, though he speaks only Arabic, and our fixer is all smiles that he has successfully helped us. This is our introduction to the welcoming and friendly Libyan people.

With our new dark green-on-white Libyan license plates, we have survived the border crossing out of Egypt and into Libya and we are on our way. We drive through the desert with glimpses of the Mediterranean on our right until we reach Tobruk, where we need money immediately as no bank issues Libyan dinars back in Egypt, and we have only a few Libyan dinars left from our money exchange on the border. After driving around for quite some time looking for an ATM, we eventually find one in the city center attached to a bank. All is sounding good as it clatters away processing our request, and the machine spits out our receipt, but from the money slot below there is nothing. The screen now reads, "Sorry, machine is out of order". Oh dear! Our receipt reads that we have just withdrawn the equivalent of AU$400! The bank is closed so there is little we can do today. Tobruk is now where we will spend the night.

We find a restaurant where a friendly elderly man speaks some English and his son even more. They are excited to help us and ask if we have any Australian pins. Unfortunately they are back in our vehicle parked a distance away. They recommend a good hotel and after checking in we go back to the restaurant and deliver our Aussie pins. They are thrilled. Australians in Tobruk are revered, we discover, and everywhere people want to shake our hands, thanks of course to the legendary Rats of Tobruk and the siege during World War II. Our hotel is the Jaghboub Hotel and the owner lends us his precious photographic history book to browse through – *The Rats Remain. The Siege of Tobruk, 1941* by J.S. Cumpston. He also encourages us to visit the war cemeteries and the Australian (Fig Tree) Hospital on our way out of Tobruk.

For dinner we walk back to our welcoming restaurant and have a pizza and Pepsi, and our elderly friend beams at us wearing his new kangaroo pin. After our meal he flatly refuses payment despite our protests. It has been a mixed day.

★★★

We glance at the ATM outside the bank the next morning – still not working – so we enter and it is full and buzzing with locals and seems chaotic. Eventually at the counter an English-speaking employee listens patiently while we try to explain our predicament, receipt in hand. He tells us to wait, so we stand to one side mistakenly believing he is looking into the situation for us. We watch him as he continues with his work behind the counter, occasionally disappearing out the back. We have learnt to be patient in these types of situations but after three quarters of an hour we realize nothing is happening. So, we protest and are shown to a back room where it seems we are talking to the manager, who assures us that the transaction from the previous day has been canceled, which is encouraging if correct, but we still need local currency.

He points to another bank across the square where we should be able to exchange US dollars for Libyan dinars. We insist he walks over with us to explain our situation and he takes us into the office of the manager who is a huge man of African descent wearing a smart suit with white shirt and tie. The manager speaks impeccable English and explains politely to us that exchanging US dollars is not recommended as it is a 'black shop' activity – we know he means black market. He suggests we try the ATMs, and when we recount our ATM experience so far he tells us to try one of the two ATMs which are strangely located over at the hospital a few kilometers away. Thankfully, he suggests we go in his car with his driver who proves to be very helpful. Incredibly there is an ATM right outside the hospital gate and a second one inside. Neither is working. The driver makes a number of phone calls in Arabic on his mobile phone for assistance in booting up the machine. Miraculously he is successful and we have our Libyan dinars in two transactions in order not to crash the precious machine. On the way back he also helps us buy a local sim phone card in a tiny shopping center. We are very grateful and he is so obliging.

With only a five day transit visa to drive the huge distance across Libya to Tunisia, we are well behind schedule, but still take the time to heed our local tour adviser. The Fig Tree Hospital was a World War II field dressing station used as a base to treat the wounded from the battleground. It is up on a rocky ridge and today consists of a lonely sprawling fig tree, where once there were many, which shades the entrance to a series of deep natural underground caves just a few kilometers from what was once the front line. The area is now surrounded by a recently constructed brick enclosure and it's hard to envisage the battles which were fought in this unforgiving stark landscape. By all accounts an off-shoot of the remaining fig tree has been planted in the gardens of

Melbourne's Shrine of Remembrance.

Twenty-five kilometers out of Tobruk is the Knightsbridge Cemetery at Acroma on the road to Benghazi. This place is out in the middle of nowhere and has a more desolate feel to it than El Alamein. Under a crisp blue sky the tall Cross of Sacrifice looms from a rise above the cemetery and can be seen clearly from the road. There are over three and a half thousand Commonwealth servicemen of World War II buried or commemorated here. There is not a soul in sight on this lonely wind-swept tract of sand now incongruously watched over by towering electricity cables. Vegetation is limited to rows of stunted palm trees and a few cactus plants with the occasional brightly colored flower punctuating the expanse of graves. We find many Australian headstones with the familiar Rising Sun badge above the dedication, but the most heartbreaking are those that read: 'FOUR AUSTRALIAN SOLDIERS OF THE 1939–1945 WAR', and inscribed under a cross: 'KNOWN UNTO GOD'. It is a somber experience.

We keep moving along the coast road, where the stony desert of rugged hills and low scrub falls into the clear blue Mediterranean under more clear blue sky. Our next stop is at Apollonia where we had planned to stay the first night. The ruins here and at nearby Cyrene are not to be missed, we have been told, so we stay at the El Manara Hotel at Apollonia, and our room overlooks the small port where newly constructed wooden boats are painted blue and sit on the dock. To the right we can see the ruins stretching from the entrance for a kilometer along the coast to the Greek Theater. Apollonia was a seaport inhabited by the Greeks as early as 700 BC and served as a harbor for the colony of Cyrene, 18 kilometers to the west. Later the Romans inhabited the city and there are also visible Byzantine influences.

We wander through impressive marble columns of both Greek and Roman origin and walk on patches of old mosaic tile floors of intricate design, still beautiful despite weathering by the elements. Along with grazing woolly sheep we stroll through arches of expert stone masonry. The Byzantine Cross is still visible etched into the stonework of the Byzantine Palace. We climb to the Greek Theater and gaze down across its semi-circular symmetry out to sea. It is still majestic and awe inspiring, and seems to welcome the sea with open arms. Some ruins of the original harbor are visible just below the shoreline, submerged as a result of earthquakes centuries ago. We are enthralled by the lack of tourists – only one other tourist whom we have met at the hotel is also exploring the site, an overlander from England who has traveled the entire coastline of Africa starting in Morocco but fears he will soon be stopped at the Algerian border.

Cyrene, a Greek colony, lies further inland high up in *Jabal al-Akhdar* (the Green Mountains) with a more distant view over the Mediterranean. This fertile, forested upland area of Libya was once known as the breadbasket of Rome and saved Greece from famine in 390 BC. It is one of the most impressive expanses of ruins in the world. The ruin of the Temple of Zeus stands larger than the Parthenon in Athens, reflecting the status of the city in the ancient Greek world. As we leave Cyrene even today it is obvious this area is important agriculturally with broad-acre farming on quite a vast plain of red fertile soil.

El Fadeel Hotel in Benghazi is where we spend the night, ready for a huge day's drive along the coast to Leptis Magna the next day. We thought fuel in Egypt was cheap but here it only costs AU$8.50 to fill a tank with diesel, a mere $0.13 per liter. A huge day's drive it is – 903 kilometers and 11 hours. The road is generally very good, sometimes with dual carriage, but often with road works. We pass a truck filled with seated camels, looking absurd with only the camels' heads and necks visible as they peer over the sides looking out in all directions. At various roadblocks we are stopped to have our papers checked, and we find it is faster if we state where we are from first, then how long we are in the country, and in no time we are waved on, sometimes not even having to show any papers at all. We see evidence of the Great Man Made River (GMR). Claimed to be the world's largest engineering venture, water is pumped from four major underground basins in the desert of southern Libya and piped across the country to supply the country's water needs.

Exhausted by the time we arrive in Leptis Magna, we find a very adequate campsite next to an old apartment building. Across the road a great local restaurant that serves up Libyan soup, fish and real couscous makes up for the lack of beer or wine in this alcohol-free part of the world and the waiters are friendly and interested in our journey. There are fewer tourists coming to Libya at the moment with the ban on tourists from Europe. Leptis Magna was once the largest and greatest Roman city in Africa, partly due to the fact that one of the Roman emperors of the time, Lucius Septimius Severus, was born there. He lavished wealth and buildings on the city and the massive Arch of Septimius Severus makes a spectacular welcome and the ruins today are impressive and unspoiled, making it easier to imagine its glorious heyday. It also has a magnificent theater overlooking the sea, and extensive, well-preserved Roman baths. We visit on a Muslim holy day which is a holiday so there are many local tourists adding to the atmosphere. They smile and wave to us and once we are asked to join a group photo.

★★★

Our GPS maps are not routable in Libya so navigating is a challenge. A destination on our GPS map is a point on the end of a straight line from our current position, which is of little help. Adding to that, every sign along the road is only in Arabic, though fortunately the Lonely Planet has each town or city printed in Arabic alongside the English, so we have a source of reference. For example, Leptis Magna starts with a circle with a stroke above it, like a head with a hat not attached, and then three strokes like the little letter 'l' above a straight-ish line. And Tripoli starts with a round U and then three tall strokes as it goes along, the last one being the stroke of what looks like a big letter 'b' at the end. But what we call first and last is really last and first in Arabic, so you can be tricked into thinking that places starting with the same sound might look the same at the 'beginning'. Of course they don't. But we do eventually find our hotel in Tripoli, despite some lively exchanges between navigator and driver.

★★★

Rule 3) Never walk or drive at night. After getting hopelessly lost in the back streets of Tripoli, it seems we should definitely review this rule. Never ever walk or drive at night.

In the twilight of our first evening in Tripoli, we walk to a restaurant not far from the Medina (old city). The Athar Restaurant seems popular with locals and occupies a beautiful setting next to the illuminated Arch of Marcus Aurelius, the only standing relic of Roman Tripoli. Seated on the terrace near the arch we sip our non-alcoholic beer and enjoy the bread and olives. Here they serve *Algarra* – a clay pot with tomato flavored sauce and some vegetables, with a choice of lamb, seafood or baby camel. Unable to bear the thought of eating baby camel – ridiculous really as we eat lamb every other day – of course we choose seafood. They bring the clay pot next to the table and by hitting it with a little hammer, break it open, releasing the piping hot food onto a waiting dinner plate. The spicy aroma is intoxicating and it's delicious, as are the steaming vegetables and couscous served as an accompaniment.

Although it is dark after dinner it seems easier to walk back to the hotel, retracing our steps through the brightly lit streets of the Medina, than try to find a taxi. So we set off confidently, but each laneway resembles the next and inevitably we take a wrong turn, and while continually trying to correct our mistake we become totally lost. Feeling vulnerable in slightly too-darkish alleyways that have become narrow with overcrowded housing and rather too many people who look rather too menacing from our current perspective, we witness a disconcerting stoush between what appears to be a couple of imported workers from East or Southern Africa. But we keep our heads down and keep walking, and try not to look anxious. Thankfully, we end up in what we later realize is the crowded and hectic bus and taxi station, and bundle into the first taxi we can find. And 'so good-to-travel-with' Brian has the hotel business card in his coat pocket, written in Arabic, so the very nice taxi driver knows exactly where to take us.

We are only a short distance from our hotel as it turns out, and the taxi driver drops us on a corner and points in the direction of our hotel. As we walk along trying to orientate ourselves, he suddenly runs up behind us and points in the opposite direction, gesturing apologetically for sending us the wrong way. The whole experience and our feeling of vulnerability is probably more perception than reality, as Tripoli at this time is reputedly a very safe and crime-free city, as no-one dares to break the law, but it is so good to be safely back in our hotel room.

★★★

We spend two nights in Tripoli at the Four Seasons Hotel in walking distance from the central Green Square as well as the Medina. The hotel, with friendly and helpful staff, has a somewhat gaudy decor of polished timber and gold trim, and massive elaborate light fittings bulging forth from the ceilings. Our room looks out over the street across a city draped in huge Gaddafi posters and green flags, with surprisingly few city lights visible at night.

The souk of the Medina has a very relaxed atmosphere with the people courteous and no aggressive selling or bartering from the merchants. No one hassles us as we stroll around the market. Brass and copper artifacts with the artisans close by working at their craft, silk fabrics and clothing embroidered with sequins and gems, jewelry, masses of scarves, rugs and colored hanging lamps adorn a variety of stalls throughout the *souk*, as well as uninspiring western clothing and furnishings. We order a coffee in an outdoor café near the white Ottoman Clock Tower and relax in the sun surrounded by old buildings and laneways and everyday life in Tripoli.

Overlooking the Medina not far away is a plush five star skyscraper, Corinthea Hotel. The 26th floor restaurant is closed but we ask if we can catch the lift up there for a view of the city.

Obligingly we are accompanied by one of the employees who waits patiently after he has given us permission to take photos. From here it is a magnificent view looking down over the Medina and the modern city beyond hugging the Mediterranean. The coffee and the selection of Arabian sweets on offer in the café downstairs is good too.

On our last night in Tripoli we eat at the al-Saraya Restaurant on Green Square. We have another great seafood meal of fried calamari and Seafood *Tajin* – with the sea so close we just can't resist.

★★★

We leave Tripoli with the usual confusion of exiting a large city. On the way to the border is the Roman city of Sabratha, yet another ancient Roman city ruin with a towering Roman Theater. By this time we could be forgiven for being 'ruined-out', but we are still fascinated with marble columns, marble floors, evidence of marble walls, old mosaic floors, and the grandeur of construction and architecture – simply 'marbleous'! The Roman theater here is mind blowing. Once having a capacity of 5,000 seats, it has a three-storey colonnaded backdrop still mostly intact and around the stage are decorative sculptural reliefs of theatrical and historical scenes.

Lulled into complacency by our helpful fixer back at the Egyptian/Libyan border, we actually spend six nights in Libya on our five day transit visa. When we mentioned how little time we had on our visa to drive across Libya, he responded, "Five days, one week, what's it matter?" Our stay is more like a week and on approaching the border at Ras Ajdir we are a little apprehensive.

When asked the number of days we have stayed in Libya, Brian answers, "One week, same as on the visa." No one questions us further and our border crossing is lengthy but smooth.

Our Libyan fast track adventure is over already.

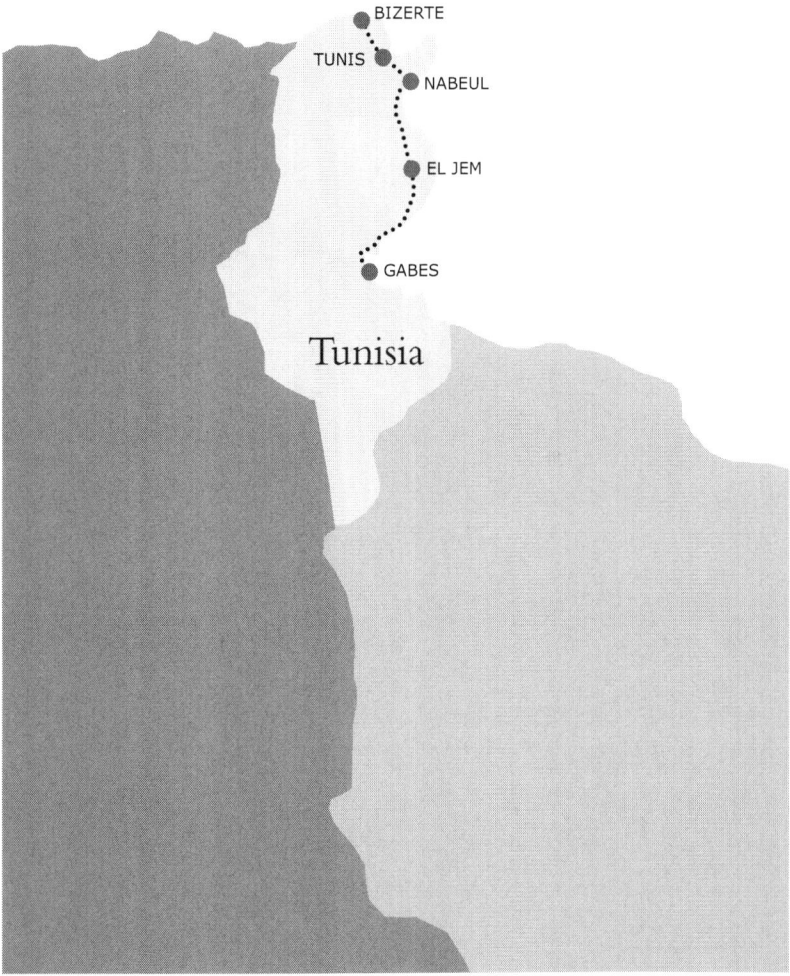

20.

Tunisia – olive oil and vineyards, gladiators, souks and Africa's northern tip

On the border into Tunisia, we have a long wait for our visa, as we have been unable to organize it before our arrival, and disappointingly the very efficient French-speaking official will not budge from issuing only a one week visa, despite our pleading and explaining our wish to see the Sahara Desert. Maybe it has been lost in translation, but only a week are we given.

Driving into Tunisia our pledge to not exchange money on borders turns out to be a mistake. To our surprise, the money spent on entry into Libya purchasing Libyan license plates for our vehicle is returned to us in Libyan dinars as we leave the country, just as we were told it would be. On the Tunisian side the money exchangers stand in the middle of the road or chase our vehicle waving money at us but we decide not to stop and exchange these unexpected Libyan dinars to Tunisian dinars. The money exchangers are very pushy and they want to take advantage of your current vulnerable situation with all the challenges of a new country.

Arriving at the first Tunisian town, we discover that Libyan dinars are definitely not the order of the day. In fact, it is a laughable proposition as far as Tunisians are concerned. Why would anyone want Libyan dinars? We continue to try to change the Libyan dinars at various banks in Tunisia, at the Tunis-Carthage International Airport (it is even more amusing for them here), and later in Palermo, Sicily when we arrive. No luck. It is not until we arrive back home that we finally sell them on eBay and without a doubt at a rate far below the offerings of the money exchangers back on the border.

With only a week in Tunisia, our first priority is to organize the ferry across to Sicily from Tunis, which we have been unable to do online. Maybe this is just as well with our shorter than anticipated stay. So in our last country on the African continent, we head north from the border towards Tunis and immediately everything feels different, as it so often does the moment a border is crossed. In this case, rather than Libya's desert landscape, we are driving through acres and acres of olive groves as far as you can see. They stand in a slightly richer-looking ploughed desert soil in neat rows up to 20 meters apart and each tree looks quite aged with a huge gnarled trunk – but obviously still productive judging by the continuous stream of roadside stalls selling plastic containers of olive oil. White washed buildings add to the Mediterranean feel of the countryside, but despite a predominantly French-speaking community, the road signs are in Arabic and thankfully also in English.

Our first night is in Gabes, where a young local walks for at least a kilometer with us to help us find the campsite just as we are about ready to give up. We feel very welcome here and enjoy a meal served at the restaurant which seems popular with the locals, and the next morning the chef unexpectedly delivers a fresh baguette and two Tom cakes after we had earlier enquired where to find fresh bread.

Traveling more inland from the Mediterranean coast, it must be slaughter-day as we see literally hundreds of sheep carcasses hanging and swaying from the beams in front of shops, in various stages of butchering. We are heading towards El-Jem and another Roman ruin, but this time to an amphitheater built in the third century, the third largest in the ancient Roman Empire, and further revealing the legacy of Roman civilization in Africa. It is worth the stop, a huge structure which has three tiers of towering colonnades and could once seat up to 30,000 people. We sit in the upper tiers on one side and imagine the excitement of a crowd enjoying the spectacle below. Chariot rides were also part of the entertainment here. We wander through the underground passages and dungeons where animals were caged and gladiators would have waited with trepidation before providing the entertainment to the masses above. Some of the scenes from 'Gladiator' starring Russell Crowe were filmed in this amphitheater. Before we leave we visit the El Jem Museum which houses a large collection of beautiful mosaics from the ancient city. Some have intricate designs and patterns, and others depict scenes of lions attacking their prey. Having been fascinated by the remains of mosaic floors in many of the ruins we have visited, is a treat to see them housed and protected with a resemblance of their former splendor.

Our destination for the night is Cap Bon, a peninsular not far from Tunis which juts out into the Mediterranean pointing towards Sicily and is a favorite tourist destination in the summer for its beaches. The drive from El-Jem is on a good road through beautifully rich agricultural country with citrus trees, vineyards and green crops, and our campsite at Nabeul in the grounds of Hotel Les Jasmines is very pleasant with a restaurant where we have a local fish meal.

We venture into Tunis the next day, finding the port in the town of Goulette, and feeling very pleased that we are able to book our ferry for the following week. North of Tunis near Bizerte we stay at a delightful old hotel called Le Petit Mousse which overlooks the Mediterranean and is better known for its restaurant than its rooms. The room is more than adequate and the restaurant perfect, it's specialty seafood. We select fresh *Loup de Mer* which is grilled and served with a bottle of Chardonnay, the first wine we have enjoyed for a long time.

Our mission the next day is to find the most northern part of the African continent, having visited the most southern point at L'Agulhas in South Africa on a previous visit, where officially the Atlantic and Indian Oceans meet. Here in Tunisia, nearly two years later, we try to find the most northern coordinates with the help of our GPS. There is nothing signposted, nothing to herald its northern-most location in any way, but quite a pretty little beach sheltered by white cliffs. Mission accomplished? Who knows? But we think it is close enough and celebrate with coffee back in Bizerte overlooking the Old Port, with its pretty blue and red fishing boats lolling against a backdrop of old stone buildings painted white or off-white with doors and windows trimmed with pale blue. An old Phoenician colony, Bizerte was also the last stronghold of the French, remaining a French base for five years after Tunisian independence in 1956.

The rest of the day we spend in Tunis which has Arabian, African, Mediterranean, Middle Eastern and European influences. Tunis features both an orderly new city of the nineteenth century created by French colonials, and an ancient and interesting Medina. An enticing souk displays the most colorful and beautiful range of goods we have yet seen in the markets. At 'Mahdaoui' beside Maytounah Mosque we have an interesting alfresco lunch. We choose one of their specialties, couscous with lamb, as we sit squashed at a restaurant table in an alleyway of the medina, chatting to a young Tunisian couple as we duck to avoid the elbows of passing pedestrians. Later we enjoy a coffee in the new city to experience the sidewalk café culture and observe how life is lived in this interesting capital. It seems a vibrant and busy place.

The next three nights we camp back at Hotel Les Jasmines which becomes packed with German tourists. Tunisia is a popular camping destination and the German tourists are catching the ferry back to Genoa and will then drive back to Germany in time for school resuming in a couple of days following the Easter holidays. We count 26 camps crammed into the campsite – all German except for two French families, one from The Netherlands and ourselves. The following morning the campsite is nearly deserted.

It is our last day in Africa. We have our last drive in Africa, and our last meal in Africa, and our last everything in Africa. Although excited to have completed the African journey and to be nearly on our way to Europe, we are sad in a way as well because we have really loved the whole African experience and after more than 35,000 kilometers, now it is nearly over. After spending a few more hours in Tunis before heading out to the port, we eventually arrive at the ferry terminal about 7 pm for our overnight trip to Palermo, Sicily, and we join the queue of vehicles and the party atmosphere waiting to board. We safely deposit Bruno, our strong and constant companion for the past eleven months, into the bowels of the vessel, and settle in to our first ever ship's cabin. The scheduled departure time is 11 pm but it is 1.30 am before the ferry glides out of the port. The lights of Tunis and Africa disappear into the darkness of the Mediterranean as we peer through our tiny porthole. What an adventure it has been.

★★★

"One's destination is never a place, but a new way of seeing things" – Henry Miller.

Visit www.jonesroadtrips.com to view more photographs

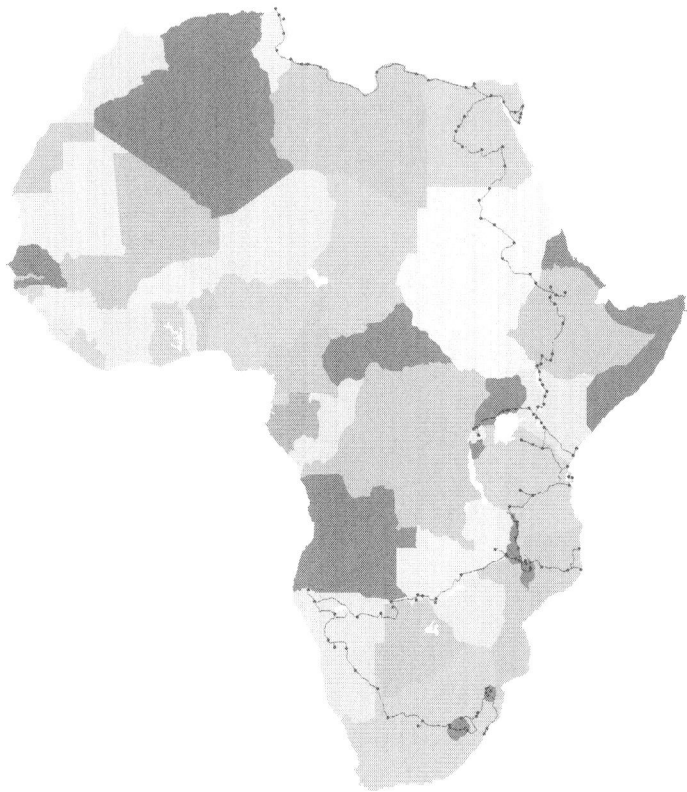

6279205R00137

Printed in Great Britain
by Amazon.co.uk, Ltd.,
Marston Gate.